The Case Management Workbook

T0231526

Defining the Role of Physicians, Nurses, and Case Managers

The Case Management Workbook

Defining the Role of Physicians, Nurses, and Case Managers

Cherilyn G. Murer, JD, CRA

Michael A. Murer, JD ◆ Lyndean L. Brick, JD

Foreword by Jill Massiet, MBA, RN

A Road Map to an Effective Integrated Health System

CRC Press
Taylor & Francis Group
Boca Raton   London   New York

CRC Press is an imprint of the
Taylor & Francis Group, an **informa** business

A PRODUCTIVITY PRESS BOOK

First published 2011 by CRC Press

Published 2019 by CRC Press
Taylor & Francis Group
6000 Broken Sound Parkway NW, Suite 300
Boca Raton, FL 33487-2742

© 2011 by Taylor & Francis Group, LLC
CRC Press is an imprint of the Taylor & Francis Group, an informa business

No claim to original U.S. Government works

ISBN-13: 978-1-4398-2777-2 (pbk)
ISBN-13: 978-1-138-43196-6 (hbk)

Visit the Taylor & Francis Web site at
http://www.taylorandfrancis.com

and the CRC Press Web site at
http://www.crcpress.com

This book is dedicated to all case managers, who are the unsung heroes of effective healthcare delivery. They push and they prod, they inform and they educate, they provide valuable information to physicians and families with a common goal—to assure the patient is provided care in the most appropriate venue correlative to the medical resources needed and provided.

Case managers are tough and resilient.

Contents

Authors' Note

This book is a sequel to *The Case Management Sourcebook: A Guide to Designing and Implementing a Centralized Case Management System,* authored by Cherilyn G. Murer, J.D., CRA, President, and Lyndean Lenhoff Brick, J.D., Senior Vice President, Murer Consultants, Inc., in 1997. This updated case management workbook reflects a number of important regulatory changes that have occurred in the past 13 years, as well as the new landscape of healthcare reform.

As with the 1997 publication, Murer Consultants believes this book will serve as an important resource for case managers, administrators, physicians and others who play a role in the case management process.

Foreword

In some small way I feel partially responsible for the idea behind the writing of this book. I met Cherilyn G. Murer, president and chief executive officer of Murer Consultants, while she was working on a project for the Baptist Health System in Little Rock, Arkansas, where I am the chief nursing officer. As part of a larger project, Cherilyn was on site conducting a work session with approximately 100 of my senior nurses.

After the presentation, Cherilyn provided me with a bound document of slides from the presentation she had just given to my staff. At that moment I told her, "Cherilyn, there is a wealth of information here. It ought to be a book." Her response was, "Jill, you know, you're right." By the end of the day Cherilyn had called her publisher, pitched the idea, and set the wheels in motion. About a month later when Cherilyn was back at our facility, she shared with me that she had laid the groundwork for this book with a focus on the role of nursing in effective case management. She asked if I would write the Foreword for this book, and of course I told her I would be honored.

During the work session that day with the nursing staff, I believe Cherilyn hit home as she pointed out the important role of nursing in the case management process. She stated that nurses interact with the patient every day and know the patient far better than anyone else. Nurses are aware of post acute venues and generally know when a patient is ready to move to the next level of care.

There are far more nurses than other health professionals in any health system, and in most cases nurses outnumber the case management staff 25 to 1. Who better to be the *eyes and ears* of case management than we, the nurses?

Not only did the presentation have an impact on me that day, but there also seemed to be an *awakening* of the nurses at our facility. As Cherilyn explained, nursing plays a pivotal role in case management. Since her presentation, there has been greater interaction between the nursing staff and the case managers. Collectively, these two groups began working as a team and, in conjunction with the physicians, began to focus on discharge planning on day one of admission.

Moving the patient appropriately not only benefits the patient but ensures that our facility is placing the right patient in the right venue at the right time for the right reimbursement. Nursing plays a critical role in the movement of our patients in a timely manner and in ensuring their care is managed effectively.

Jill Massiet, MBA, RN
Chief Nursing Officer
Baptist Health Medical Center
Little Rock, Arkansas

Acknowledgments

This book is a compendium of experiences and ideas garnered over the past 25 years. It reflects the struggles and successes of hospitals and health systems, government and other third-party payers, doctors, nurses, clinicians, and administrators who work every day to better the American health delivery system.

This book reflects the endeavors of Murer Consultants and each staff member who has worked side by side with healthcare industry providers to enhance the system.

Many individuals assisted in the shaping of the ideas and solutions reflected in this book. Special acknowledgment to Debra Frost, senior analyst, whose career has spanned more than 20 years with Murer Consultants and whose diligence and attentiveness to clients and details are reflected in the content of this book.

And no book ever gets to market without the support, patience, and prodding of the editor in charge. Kristine Mednansky has been a friend and editor to these authors for more than 15 years. She is gifted in her approach and ability to shepherd a project through publication. Many thanks to Kris and Productivity Press.

Introduction: A Genesis of Case Management

Case management has become one of the most effective means by which a continuum of care functions effectively and efficiently. The practice of case management incorporates the process of evaluating and coordinating a patient's condition and directing the patient to the most appropriate care venue based on medical necessity.

In 1997, Murer Consultants wrote its first book on case management, *The Case Management Sourcebook: A Guide to Designing and Implementing a Centralized Case Management System*. At the time the book was written, case management as a component of an integrated healthcare system was still in its infancy. The case manager generally focused on the acute inpatient revenue. As case management morphed over the past decade, the intent was to develop a model that focused on managing the patient's episode of care across a complex and diverse continuum. Implementing this model of case management has been painstakingly slow. Thirteen years later, we are dealing with many of the same issues and challenges related to ensuring the patient is in the right place at the right time for the right reimbursement.

Case management continues to be at the forefront in most health system efforts to reduce cost and ensure quality of care delivery. Case managers and the case management system are called upon to reduce the number of days a patient stays in the inpatient bed. Hospital administrators are convinced that if the length of stay is reduced, then their costs will be reduced. Although this is true to some extent, length of stay is not the only factor that negatively affects a health system's bottom line.

Myriad factors contribute to the rising cost of caring for the patient. One example is the overutilization of consulting physicians and the refusal of attending physicians to act as quarterback. Someone needs to take responsibility to ensure that the patient is not sitting in a hospital bed unnecessarily waiting for someone to say, "Hey, it's OK to move the patient to the next level of care."

Another factor is the availability of ancillary services in the evening and on weekends. Limited availability of these services not only can cause excessive inpatient days but also can result in a delay in treatment. Waiting until the next morning or waiting from Friday afternoon until Monday morning for an MRI or CT scan can no longer be tolerated as our society moves to rein in unnecessary cost in the American healthcare delivery system.

In this era of health reform, it is imperative that the case management team think outside the box, determine issues affecting the timely movement of patients, and identify solutions that intertwine organizational behavior and outcome management.

Don't just be a problem identifier—be a problem solver.

Murer Consultants' first book on case management offers guidance for healthcare managers who are trying to lead their facilities through the complicated world of healthcare. It discusses the importance of case management in the continuum of care and provides models of case management. The book provides a road map for understanding, developing, and implementing case management strategies.

However, in today's world of regulatory change, the road map must be continually redesigned and realigned. One of the greatest challenges in healthcare today is the lack of consistency in federal regulations and guidelines. This instability makes it difficult for hospitals and health systems to plan for the future. But nevertheless, the challenges must be met.

Case in point: long-term acute care hospitals (LTACHs) have been in existence since the early 1980s. There was a surge in the development of LTACHs in the late 1990s and for the next several years into the new millennium, increasing from 91 facilities in 1991 to more than 400 facilities today. Congress has supported this venue as evidenced over the past several years by increasing the base rate from $34,956 in 2003 to $39,896 in rate year (RY) 2010.

LTACHs are the only venue of care specifically designed and compensated for those medically complex patients with extended care needs. Yet the government's implementation of the 25 percent referral limitation and its three-year moratorium on any new LTACHs or additional beds in 2007 sent a mixed message to the healthcare industry. The moratorium was again extended for an additional two years with the passage of the 2010 health reform bill.

With limited beds and restrictions placed on referrals from its acute care hospitals, case managers were left scrambling for placement for their very sick patients. Many healthcare systems are forced to refer outside their own continuum because of this arbitrary referral percentage.

Managing patient care in today's healthcare environment will take a concerted effort on the part of the entire case management team—not just a handful of case managers. But as this book will emphasize, the case management team includes many more individuals than simply those with the title of care manager. A health system can no longer rely on a small, designated group of case managers devoted and dedicated to moving the patient through the continuum.

The team must consist of key clinical personnel including the nurse, the physician, and the case manager, each of whom has a specific role in case management. Administration also plays an important role. The administrator must judiciously ensure that each member of the team is on board with the hospital's or health system's goal that the patient is at the right place at the right time at each episode of care.

This book is an attempt to define the roles of the case management team and provide an overview of key post acute venues of care. Chapter 1 begins the journey of defining effective case management by providing an overview of case management, its structure, and the responsibility of each member of the case management team.

We will also learn that a key byproduct of an effective case management system is the realization of an effective integrated health system whereby physicians and hospitals are aligned as caretakers of finite health resources.

About the Authors

Cherilyn G. Murer, JD, CRA, Founder, President and Chief Executive Officer of the Murer Group, has long been an active voice in the advancement of quality, cost-effective healthcare. Ms. Murer received a juris doctor degree with honors from Northern Illinois University (NIU) and has coupled her background in law with her previous operational experience as the Director of Rehabilitation Medicine at Northwestern Memorial Hospital, Chicago, Illinois. Ms. Murer is a sought-after lecturer and educator whose focus is on assisting her clients navigate through the complex regulatory, strategic, and financial issues facing healthcare today.

In May 2005, Ms. Murer received a gubernatorial appointment, with Senate confirmation, to a six-year term on the Northern Illinois University Board of Trustees. In 2007, Ms. Murer was elected Chairman of the Board of this state university with over 26,000 students. Ms. Murer and her husband, Michael, have provided a philanthropic gift to NIU to establish the **Murer Initiative** as a forum for scholarly discussion, policy analysis and cross-disciplinary integration of medicine, law, technology, and finance. In September 2007, Ms. Murer was selected by the university to present the first Annual Executive Speaker Series Presentation, "Conversation with a CEO," co-sponsored by NIU College of Engineering and College of Business. In 2002, Ms. Murer was appointed to the Northern Illinois University Law School's prestigious Board of Visitors and was honored with its 2003 College of Law Distinguished Alumni Award. Ms. Murer holds an appointment to the faculty of the University of Illinois at Chicago College of Medicine as a Clinical Assistant Professor of Law in the Department of Family Medicine.

Coinciding with the firm's 25th anniversary (February 2010), Ms. Murer was honored by both the University of Illinois at Chicago and Northern Illinois University. On February 25, 2010, she was inducted into the prestigious Chicago Entrepreneurship Hall of Fame. In April she received the 2010 Northern Illinois University Distinguished Alumni of the Year Award, the highest award given by the NIU Alumni Association to one individual each year who has achieved national, regional, or statewide prominence.

Ms. Murer was pleased to accept, in October 2004, an invitation from the Commission on Accreditation of Rehabilitation Facilities (CARF) to participate in an International Advisory Committee on the development of the first set of International Stroke Rehabilitation Standards. Ms. Murer has presented the keynote address at the Annual Case Management Society of America Convention in Anaheim, California. As a featured speaker, she highlighted the critical role of case management in a reformed healthcare environment. Ms. Murer has been appointed by CARF to its International Advisory Committee to promote globalization of accreditation standards.

Ms. Murer has co-authored with Lyndean Lenhoff Brick and Michael A. Murer four books published by McGraw-Hill. *The Case Management Sourcebook* is a 300-page text that serves as a guide to designing and implementing a centralized case management system. A second book, published by McGraw Hill and co-published by HFMA, entitled *Post Acute Care Reimbursement Manual: A Financial and Legal Guide*, addressed the financial impact to post acute venues pre- and post-Balanced Budget Act (BBA). A third book, *Compliance Audits and Plans for Healthcare*, was one of the first books to address complex heathcare compliance issues. A fourth book, *Healthcare Records Management* is an 800-page complete guide to disclosure, retention, and technology. A fifth book was published in April of 2003 by Commerce Clearing House, Inc. (CCH), entitled *Understanding Provider-Based Status.*

As commencement speaker at her alma mater, Marymount University in Arlington, Virginia, Ms. Murer was awarded the Mother Gerard Phelan Gold Medal; previous recipients have included Nancy Reagan, the Honorable Clare Boothe Luce, Elinor Guggenheimer, and past U.S. Surgeon General, Dr. Antonia Novello. Ms. Murer was also honored by American Express; recognized for her leadership and outstanding accomplishments. American Express described Ms. Murer as "a health-care pioneer who has been a leader in helping healthcare providers find cost effective procedures without reducing the quality of care."

From April 2004 to June 2008, Ms. Murer was President of the Board of Managers of Oak Tree Hospital at Baptist Regional Medical Center in Corbin, Kentucky. She was Vice President of the Corbin Long Term Acute Care Venture, LLC Board, for the same period of time. She also served on like Boards in the same positions for Oak Tree Hospital at Baptist Northeast in LaGrange, Kentucky, and on the Northeast Joint Venture, LLC Board, from June 2006 to September 2009.

In March 2005, Ms. Murer was featured on the cover of *Modern Healthcare Magazine* with a lead story on the need for national standardization of Medicare regulations. Ms. Murer has been a columnist for

Rehab Management Magazine since 1993. Her column "Issues and Trends" focuses on timely and sometimes controversial subjects impacting the delivery of healthcare. Ms. Murer has authored over 160 articles published in journals and magazines on healthcare finance, regulatory compliance, new business development, and globalization.

Ms. Murer has developed specialized expertise in proton therapy serving as Chair of the Northern Illinois Proton Therapy and Research Center; a project in conjunction with Fermilab and Argonne National Laboratory. Her concern for the future direction of healthcare within our country prompted her to accept an appointment by Vice President George Bush to serve as National Co-Chair, Disability Coalition. She was subsequently appointed as President Bush's National Co-Chair "Access to Opportunity Committee" and served as a member of the U.S. International Cultural and Trade Center Commission Advisory Committee on Foreign Language Needs of Business.

Michael A. Murer, JD, is Executive Vice President and General Counsel for the Murer Group. Mr. Murer received his juris doctor degree from Georgetown University Law Center in Washington, D.C. and earned his Bachelor of Arts degree in European History at Purdue University in West Lafayette, Indiana.

Mr. Murer's area of expertise includes interfacing healthcare management with the changing regulatory environment. He has written and lectured extensively in the areas of compliance, electronic medical records, e-commerce, safe harbors, fraud and abuse, the Stark Laws and the structuring of joint ventures and HIPAA. Some of his lectures include "Advancing Technology and the Medical Record" at the Healthcare Informatics Expo and Conference in Chicago, Illinois; "HIPAA and E-Commerce" at the Healthcare Financial Management Association (HFMA) Annual Conference in San Antonio, Texas; "HIPAA Mapping and Plotting," for the Illinois Association of Health Plans/RX 2000 Institute in Chicago, Illinois; and most recently "How to Train Your Staff on HIPAA Privacy," for Eli Research teleconference.

Mr. Murer has been a member of the Legal Work Group for Health Information Security & Privacy Collaboration (HISPC)–Illinois II since 2007. This group worked on developing a model uniform patient Electronic Health Record (EHR)/Health Information Exchange (HIE) consent form for possible use by the state-level HIE, clinicians, healthcare facilities and other providers. The Legal Work Group was also tasked with the development of a plan to disseminate the consent form and encourage its use. In July 2009, the group was absorbed by the Illinois Health Information Exchange Advisory Committee.

Mr. Murer served as Assistant Treasurer/Secretary on the Boards of Managers for two Long Term Acute Care Hospitals in Kentucky, as well as each hospital's Joint Venture Board. From April 2004 to June 2006, he served in these positions for Oak Tree Hospital at Baptist Regional Medical Center as well as the Corbin Long Term Acute Care Venture, LLC. He was also appointed to the same positions for Oak Tree Hospital at Baptist Northeast in LaGrange, Kentucky, as well as serving on that hospital's Northeast Joint Venture, LLC Board of Managers from June 2006 to September 2009.

Mr. Murer has also served as Executive Vice President of International Healthcare Recruiting, a venture with the University of Utrecht, The Free University of Louvain and other Dutch, Belgian, and Swiss Universities in addressing international recruitment and placement of physical therapists.

Mr. Murer has been a practicing attorney for over thirty-two years and has held faculty appointments at both the graduate and undergraduate levels at Lewis University, Lockport, Illinois and the Graduate Program of St. Francis College in Health Administration in Joliet, Illinois. He was also the 1982 Congressional candidate for the U.S. Congress from the 4th Illinois District.

Mr. Murer has written numerous articles and white papers regarding the legal implications of Industrial Medicine Programs and several articles detailing the complexity associated with networks and alliances. Some of his articles include: "Embracing System Integration," *Continuing Care Magazine;* "Old Reg's Can Hamper New Healthcare Entities," *Hospital Rehab Magazine;* "Healthcare's Added Burden: The Legal System Integration in Healthcare Network and Alliances," *Hospital Rehab Magazine;* "Case Management Challenges in Integrated Health Systems," *Continuing Care;* and "A.G. (After Globalization)" published in the *San Francisco Business Times.* Additionally, Mr. Murer served from 1990 to 1992 as editor of *Year Magazine,* a news magazine examining the upcoming decade of change. One of Mr. Murer's latest articles, "Compliance Guidance for Nursing Facility Caregivers," was published in *CCH Healthcare Compliance Letter.* In addition, he recently became a member of the CCH Healthcare Compliance Editorial Advisory Board.

Mr. Murer is a leading advocate of e-commerce and technology. He was the lead developer of ComplianceEdge, an interactive Internet compliance-training program for hospitals and health systems; a product developed by Murer Consultants, Inc., for CCH, Inc., and Ernst & Young. He also worked on an upper management web-based tool developed with Aon Corporation.

Lyndean Lenhoff Brick, JD, is the Senior Vice President with the Murer Group. She received her juris doctor degree from The Ohio State University College of Law. Since that time, she has been actively engaged in Healthcare Law and Management Consulting.

Ms. Brick's practice is concentrated on healthcare law including Medicare/Medicaid regulation and reimbursement; healthcare compliance; HIPAA compliance; Certificate of Need development and review; corporate restructuring, joint ventures, acquisitions and capital formation; reimbursement review and TEFRA structuring; managed healthcare and regulation; and risk management for healthcare facilities. Ms. Brick has lectured on a variety of health-related topics including Case Management, Provider-Based Regulations; HIPAA; Compliance and CORF development. The Healthcare Financial Management Association (HFMA) honored Ms. Brick with their Annual National Institute's (ANI) Distinguished Speaker Award in 2002 and 2003. She is nationally recognized for her work and client representation in the field of Medicare and Medicaid rules and regulations. She is the regulatory lead counsel to a national base of clients and has served as the acting CEO of a fourteen-chain hospital system in Texas and Louisiana.

Ms. Brick also consults in the areas of strategic and long-range planning for healthcare providers and regularly advises clients in the assessment and development of joint venture opportunities in the healthcare industry. Additionally, she works on the feasibility of development for alternative sites of care such as Ambulatory Surgery Centers (ASCs) and Independent Diagnostic Testing Facilities (IDTFs).

Ms. Brick additionally has significant experience in assisting providers with emergency disaster preparation and recovery. Ms. Brick works with providers individually to ensure that requisite policies and procedures are implemented and in place in anticipation of emergency disasters to ensure optimal reimbursement potential from Federal and State sources of funding. Based on her experiences with past disasters, most recently Hurricanes Gustav, Ike, Katrina, and Rita, Ms. Brick has gained beneficial insight as to Federal disaster reimbursement processes and what measures need to be taken before, during, and after a disaster occurs to promote a provider's eligibility for reimbursement.

Ms. Brick also has considerable operational experience in the health-care industry, having been the contract Administrative Director of a 42-bed inpatient rehabilitation unit in Johnson City, Tennessee, and Contract Manager of program development for a 175,000-square-foot out-patient healthcare facility in Canada. In June 2005, Ms. Brick received a gubernatorial appointment to serve as a member of the Illinois Hospital Licensing Board and has since been elected the Board's Chairperson. Ms. Brick was appointed as one of two members of the board representing governing bodies of hospitals. She serves on the Regional Board of Provena Saint Joseph Medical Center Board of Directors in Joliet, Illinois and is the Finance Chair of the hospital and became the secretary of the Provena divisional Board in 2009. Ms. Brick also was appointed by Will County Executive Larry Walsh to the Will County Health Department Board.

She has contributed to such healthcare newsletters as *Eli Research* and *CCH Healthcare Compliance Letter.* One of her most recent articles for the *CCH Healthcare Compliance Letter* was titled "Independent Diagnostic Testing Facilities (IDTFs): A Good Way to Cooperate."

Prior to joining Murer Consultants, Inc. Ms. Brick worked as an inter-national attorney with a particular expertise in German. As a business consultant in Chicago, Illinois, her responsibilities included the negotia-tion and formation of international healthcare joint ventures, medical product development, international marketing and market research, commercial and regulatory law, and capital formation.

Ms. Brick has considerable experience in the formation and operation of foreign-based healthcare clinics as well as in guiding international clients through marketing and the American regulatory process.

1

Who Is Responsible for Case Management?

OVERVIEW

Gone are the days where a patient remains in the hospital simply for the sake of physician or family convenience. Hospitals cannot survive operating under the mentality of a five-day work week. If the patient is ready for discharge on Friday at 3:00 p.m., a system must be in place to move the patient to the next level of care, be it skilled nursing, inpatient rehabilitation, long-term acute care hospital, home health, or hospice (see Figure 1.1).

Hospitals can no longer tolerate the adage "If it's Friday afternoon you can bet nothing's happening until Monday," or weekends being referred to as "the weekend protection program." Yet hospitals across the nation can relate to both of these issues. In many hospitals, it's a well-known fact that if arrangements are not made by Friday morning to discharge the patient to either another level of care or home, then the patient is not going anywhere until Monday. By Friday afternoon the attending physician is gone for the weekend, and it is unlikely that the physician on call will provide

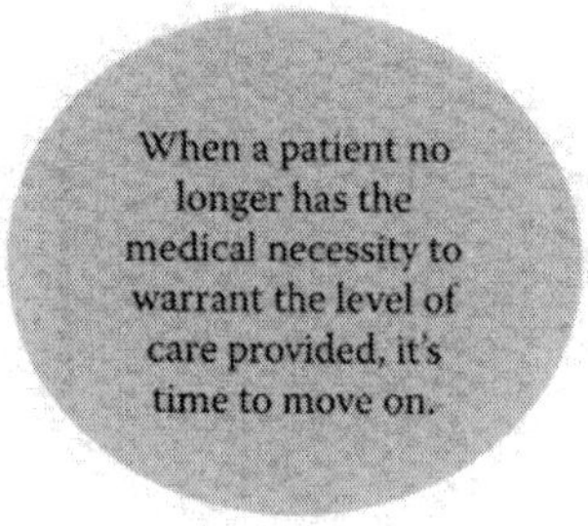

> When a patient no longer has the medical necessity to warrant the level of care provided, it's time to move on.

FIGURE 1.1
It's time to move on.

anything but overnight care over the weekend. The patient remains in a virtual "physician protected program" until the weekend is over.

These additional days are extremely costly. Acute hospitals are paid by Centers for Medicare and Medicaid Services (CMS) under the inpatient prospective payment system (IPPS). This system applies specific diagnostic-related groups (DRGs) to each discharge. Each DRG has an arithmetic mean length of stay (AMLOS), which is the average number of days patients within that DRG classification stay in the hospital. When a patient stays beyond the AMLOS, the hospital is basically providing care to its Medicare population for which they are no longer being compensated, also referred to as uncompensated care.

WHAT IS UNCOMPENSATED CARE?

Uncompensated care is equal to the amount that exceeds capitation under the prospective payment system. It represents the amount of care non-reimbursed by Medicare. The DRG system may be used as a benchmark in which, through experience and customary usage, it has been determined that managed care, through its negotiations with the provider, generally will not exceed the per diem paid by Medicare.

For example, Medicare pays $5,000 for a specific DRG that has a projected length of stay of five days. If a patient stays seven days, he accumulates two days of uncompensated care totaling $2,000 (see Figure 1.2).

If a patient is moved appropriately, there is bed turnover. Bed turnover is the amount the facility will generate in new money once an acute bed

Full DRG Payment = $5,000

AMLOS = 5 Days

Average Daily Per Diem = $1,000

Full Payment for Five Days = $5,000

Two Days/Uncompensated Care = −$2,000

FIGURE 1.2
Example uncompensated care.

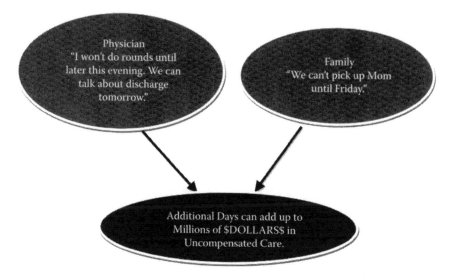

FIGURE 1.3
Examples of reasons the patient is not moved.

becomes available. If the hospital does not fill the bed, it will at least not have the cost associated with the bed.

With effective case management, the hospital can mitigate uncompensated care and generate new revenues through utilization of alternative post acute venues of care. Effective case management also presents the opportunity to turn over the acute bed with a new patient, resulting in stable revenues and rightly sizing up the number of acute beds.

There are all kinds of reasons to not move the patient (see Figure 1.3). For example, the patient's family states they don't have transportation today to take the patient home but they can make arrangements for tomorrow. It may be that the physician rounds late and therefore the patient waits until the next morning to move to the next level of care. From both a regulatory and a financial perspective, it is imperative that patients are moved in a timely manner.

MOVING THE PATIENT IN A TIMELY MANNER

Post acute venues, when used appropriately, can mitigate the revenue loss of patients staying beyond the DRG length of stay. Post acute venues afford the referring hospital the opportunity to capture additional revenue by turning over the acute bed in a timely fashion.

However, to minimize uncompensated care loss, the health system must have the post acute venues available to move the patient throughout the continuum. Identifying and moving patients in a timely manner can do a number of things:

1. It reduces the referring hospital's uncompensated care loss.
2. It allows for additional bed turnover at the referring hospital.
3. It increases the number of patients at the next post acute venue for an additional payment to the health system.

When Medicare, Medicaid, or a private payer is responsible for payment, it is critical that patients meet the medical criteria to warrant the care they are receiving in the specific venue. When a patient no longer has the medical necessity for a specific venue of care, it is time to move on. Hospitals and healthcare systems must be prudent with their healthcare dollars. Leaving patients in a venue for which they are no longer appropriate for the sake of convenience is wrong!

We as a country are being called upon to reform healthcare. In May 2009, some of the healthcare industry's top leaders pledged to cut approximately $2 trillion in healthcare costs over a 10-year period. Reducing the cost of healthcare will require streamlined care, a focus on quality and efficiency, better coordination of care, adherence to evidence-based practices, and better use of healthcare information technology (see Figure 1.4).

Quality and efficiency can no longer be just a slogan. They must become a reality. It seems every community has a top hospital; in fact there are hundreds of "Top 100 Hospitals."

Streamlining care:	Focus on outpatient and ambulatory care
Focusing on quality and efficiencies:	Not only a slogan
Better care coordination:	Interface of physician and hospital
Adhering to evidence-based best practices:	Great idea!
Better utilizing health information technology:	Costly and complex but avenue to best long-range cost containment

FIGURE 1.4
Top objectives to reduce healthcare costs. (*Source:* Murer Consultants, Inc.)

Hospitals across the country tout that they are among the top hospitals. But what defines a top hospital? In many instances one must delve down deep to understand what makes a hospital a leader in a specific area or percentile. For example, were the criteria based on predetermined national benchmarks? Were they based on patient satisfaction scores? Is the award a national one, or is the facility the top hospital in its specific community or state? Is the hospital itself number one, or is this rating based on a specific product line? Was the award broken out by classes according to bed size, community versus urban, or national versus state? These are all factors a hospital can base its notoriety upon.

THE USE OF THE EMERGENCY DEPARTMENT

With a sinking economy, there are fewer people insured. Elective surgeries are down. With large numbers of people out of work, many are turning to emergency departments for their healthcare needs. At some institutions, charity care is up to 20 percent, forcing the hospital to closely watch every healthcare dollar.

The practice of using the emergency room for nonemergency issues must stop. Individuals need to make preventive office visits and choose clinics or immediate care facilities rather than rushing to the emergency room with colds or minor conditions.

In the American Hospital Association's (AHA) 2010 edition of its hospital statistics, based on comprehensive data on hospital trends from the 2008 AHA Annual Survey, the AHA reported U.S. hospitals handle more than 123 million patients with emergency needs. This was an increase of 2 million visits since 2007.

This trend seems poised to continue. It is projected that even as the economy improves and more individuals return to work, many will be considered the *working poor*, and as we implement health reform with 32 million people to be insured, providers have an enhanced incentive to ensure judicious use of resources.

With less available healthcare dollars it will be more important than ever to ensure that patients move effectively through the system. Case management will be called upon to ensure that patients move appropriately from acute to post acute venues of care.

THE ESSENCE OF EFFECTIVE CASE MANAGEMENT

What system can a healthcare organization rely upon to ensure appropriate throughput of patient care? *Case management.* Case management is the appropriate and effective movement of patients along the continuum of care. Who is responsible for case management? Everyone:

- physicians
- nurses
- administrators
- case managers

These key individuals must work as a team to ensure that admission criteria and discharge triggers are followed for the various venues of care to allow for appropriate and judicious use of resources.

Communication between the key players is the essence of effective case management (see Figure 1.5).

1. The nurse initiates the process.
2. The physician authorizes the process.
3. The case manager implements the process.
4. Administration oversees the process and ensures that each team member adheres to the protocols put in place.

To be effective, case management must have the cooperation of all team members and a concerted effort among the parties to ensure that

FIGURE 1.5
Everyone has a responsibility in case management.

the patient appropriately utilizes the healthcare continuum. It's essential that all team members have a working knowledge and understanding of the regulatory and financial implications of patients staying beyond the intended length of stay.

Each team member must

- focus on the appropriate outcomes to reduce the length of stay;
- focus on meaningful duties;
- become a problem solver, not simply a problem identifier;
- effectively articulate obstacles; and
- be less process oriented and more outcome focused.

Everyone responsible for case management must

- ensure that a general understanding of the healthcare industry is maintained. It is essential to remain current especially during this era of revised regulations as health reform evolves. Watch TV, read the newspaper, surf the Web, and discuss these issues with colleagues in the workplace and in the community.
- be knowledgeable of the functional uses and admission criteria of the various venues of care. The team must be fluent in articulating discharge triggers to the next level of care.
- be familiar with the regulatory requirements pertaining to each post acute venue. For example:
  - Medical necessity—Is a long-term acute care hospital the ideal venue for a patient with a wound?
  - Home care—If the family isn't able to drive the patient to rehab, then is the patient really homebound from a Medicare perspective?
- have a general understanding of the reimbursement structure for each specific venue and payer.

STRUCTURE

The following section outlines the structure of the case management team and targets responsibilities of each of the team members involved in the management of the patient through the integrated health system.

PHYSICIAN'S RESPONSIBILITY

- Commitment
- Leadership
- Self-Education

FIGURE 1.6
Physician's responsibility.

Physician

The physician must be committed to an effective and efficient healthcare delivery system appropriately utilizing all tools and resources available. The physician must provide leadership in the timely and appropriate use of any specialty unit (e.g., ICU or telemetry beds) and post acute venues (i.e., long-term acute care hospital, skilled nursing, rehab).

It is the physician's responsibility to be self-educated regarding the options of each major venue of care relevant to his or her medical specialty. Furthermore, the physician's involvement in ensuring that the patient is in the right place at the right time will be more prevalent in the future if the government begins bundling a patient's stay and the physician payment under an acute episode of care (see Figure 1.6).

Note: This scenario where the physician and the hospital will each receive a portion of a fixed amount will be explained in Chapter 2.

Nursing

Nurses are on the front line, dealing with physicians, the patient, and the patient's family on a daily basis. It is important that the nurse be the *eyes and ears* of case management.

Nurses interact with their patients every day. Nurses instinctively know when it's time to consider moving the patient. It is important that nurses be aware of the anticipated discharge destination when the patient is admitted.

Nurses also need a general understanding of the purpose of each venue and the discharge triggers to the next venue of care. Nursing is the guiding light of case management. Case managers depend upon the nursing staff for cues as to the timeliness of discharge from acute care and admission to post acute venues depending on medical needs of the patient (see Figure 1.7).

SO WHAT'S A NURSE TO DO?

- Be the eyes and ears of case management.
- Be aware of anticipated discharge destination at time of patient admission to unit.

Nursing is the guiding light for case management.

FIGURE 1.7
Nurses' responsibility.

CASE MANAGER'S RESPONSIBILITY

- Choreographer of resource utilization.
- Knowledgeable of all post acute venues, including regulatory, financial, and operational distinctions.

FIGURE 1.8
Case manager's responsibility.

Case Managers

The case manager is the choreographer of resource utilization and must be knowledgeable of the available menu of service delivery modes and environments (see Figure 1.8).

Administration

Occasionally a member of the case management team will run into a physician who is not "with the program." When this happens the nurse or case manager must rely on strong administrative support. The staff must be confident that administration will back them up and support any further action needed to be taken against a "problem physician" (see Figure 1.9)

If the nurse initiates, the physician authorizes, and the case manager implements, it is imperative that administration oversees the process and ensures that everyone has the tools to work together toward a common goal. It will take the concerted effort of these key stakeholders to ensure that patients are appropriately moved through the continuum of care.

> ### ADMINISTRATION'S RESPONSIBILITY
>
> - Oversee physician buy-in.
> - Back up staff as appropriate.

FIGURE 1.9
Administration's responsibility.

Everyone

The case management team must be knowledgeable in all aspects of the continuum. Each individual must be aware of the subtle differences relative to purpose of venue, admission requirements, intended length of stay, and reimbursement expectations.

CASE MANAGEMENT IS TRULY EVERYONE'S RESPONSIBILITY

The most difficult hurdle to overcome in ensuring the patient is moved appropriately through the system is the misalignment of financial incentives. The physician and the hospital are paid differently. There are conflicting financial incentives in place today. Chapter 2 examines the misalignment of the two parties.

> ### CHAPTER 1 ACTION ITEMS
>
> - Define key players on your case management team.
> - What elements are contributing to your facility's loss of potential revenues?
> - Ensure that the case management team has the necessary common language and common knowledge to be effective.

2

Financial Incentives

ALIGNING INCENTIVES: CURRENT PAYMENT STRUCTURE

The American healthcare payment system is out of alignment. Part of the problem in moving the patient appropriately through the system is the way our government compensates differently for those providing care.

Medicare pays healthcare providers fixed amounts for each service provided to beneficiaries. Medicare administers one payment system for short-term acute care hospitals and other payment methods for post acute care venues including the comprehensive inpatient rehabilitation unit/facility, the skilled nursing unit/facility, the long-term acute care hospital, outpatient, and home healthcare. Nonsurgical physicians are paid each time they see the patient. The more contact they have with the patient, the more they are compensated.

The Physician Payment

With today's Medicare system, the physician is paid each time he or she has contact with the patient. In an acute care hospital, this means on a daily basis. Physicians are reimbursed under the Medicare Physician Fee Schedule for each service they perform. Under this payment structure, physicians are incentivized to keep patients beyond the anticipated length of stay under their projected diagnosis-related group (DRG). In fact, some believe this creates a financial incentive for unnecessary treatment. Physicians are not penalized for keeping their patients too long. This burden falls on the hospital or health system, which receives a single prospective payment based on diagnoses.

DRG Weight × Hospital Base Rate = Individual DRG Payment
1.4796 × $5,300 = $7,841.88

FIGURE 2.1
Example: Determining payment for DRG 193.

Hospital Payments

Hospitals are paid under the inpatient prospective payment system, which applies DRGs to determine hospital reimbursement. The Centers for Medicare and Medicaid (CMS) determine DRG payments based on historical data using the average length of stay and the resources used on a case-by-case basis.

Each year, based on this historical information, CMS publishes anticipated lengths of stay and weights. The individual weights are then applied each year to the facility's base rate to determine payment. The hospital's base rate is applied to each Medicare discharge and is the basis for the DRG payment. The base rate is adjusted based on a geographical factor, which measures the cost of labor in each local area as well as other issues including the location, rural or urban designation, and other issues.

For example, let's say Hospital A has a Medicare base rate this year of $5,300. To determine the payment for a patient with DRG 193, Simple Pneumonia and Pleurisy with MCC (major complication/comorbidity), you would take DRG 193's relative weight, which for 2011 is 1.4796, and multiply it by Hospital A's base rate to arrive at the facility-based payment for DRG 193, which in this case would be $7,841.88 (see Figure 2.1).

Post Acute Venue Payments

When patients are discharged from a short-term acute care hospital to a post acute venue, a new admission is triggered. Thus, the post acute venue will receive a new payment for the care it administers based upon the relevant post acute payment system.

The Medicare fee-for-service program pays post acute providers a fixed amount for each service provided to beneficiaries. Each post acute venue is paid differently. For example, inpatient rehabilitation facilities are paid under case mix groups (CMGs). Skilled nursing facilities are paid under resource utilization groups (RUGs). Long-term acute care hospitals are paid under long-term care diagnosis-related groups (LTC-DRGs). Each post acute venue or service has its own Medicare payment structure.

Specific reimbursement details associated with these post acute venues are explained in more detail in Chapter 6.

FRAUD AND ABUSE

The U.S. government spends billions each year on fraudulent payments for Medicare and Medicaid service errors. Although these errors may not be intentional, they are nonetheless costing our country precious healthcare dollars. Therefore, it is the goal of our government to put a halt to the billions of federal dollars lost as a result of improper payments.

The current practice of insurance companies is to scrutinize the admission process and to ensure that patients truly need the care they are receiving and have demonstrated the medical necessity to require this level of care, and now the federal government is beginning to take on this same practice. The government has begun to take a close look at the care being administered to ensure that the patient has the medical necessity to require a certain level of care. They are also looking at the payment postdischarge under the Recovery Audit Contractors (RAC) program to retroactively ensure no improper payment was made.

The federal government is also looking at ways to bundle payments, combining the hospital and physician payment and/or combining the short-term acute stay with the post acute payment. The following section is an overview of audits in place and future proposed bundling incentive payments.

RECOVERY AUDIT CONTRACTORS AUDITS

The CMS is now looking closely at patients post-discharge. At the direction of Congress, CMS designed the RAC program to detect and correct past improper payments in the Medicare fee-for-service program and to help prevent future improper payments. The RAC demonstration project began in 2005 and ended in March 2008. Section 302 of the Tax Relief and Healthcare Act of 2006 directed the Secretary of Health and Human Services to make the RAC program permanent and nationwide by January 1, 2010.

CMS is currently in the process of expanding the demonstration program to be permanent in all 50 states and has four RACs in place. Each

RAC is responsible for identifying overpayments and underpayments in approximately 25 percent of the country. Unfortunately for the provider, the focus is again on the facility—not the physician. However, although RAC does not address the facility/physician misalignment, this issue is addressed in a proposed bundling structure.

FUTURE PAYMENT STRUCTURE

CMS is examining the way it pays hospitals, physicians, and post acute care providers. Several proposals are currently on the table and will be discussed in this section.

Bundling Physician and Hospital Payments

One of the proposals has Medicare bundling the short-term acute hospital payment with the physician payment. CMS is currently conducting demonstration projects for the acute care episode (ACE). The goal of the ACE demonstration is to use a bundled payment to better align the incentives for the hospital and the physician in an effort to provide better quality and greater efficiency in the care that is provided.

Under the current system, the physician is paid based on the number of services or procedures performed. If the physician has contact with the patient, a payment is made. The hospital receives one payment under the DRG system. This demonstration project looked at the effect of a single bundled payment on the services provided.

The ACE demonstration project began in 2009 and is slated to run through 2012. Five locations are taking part in this project. The focus of the pilot project is on high-volume procedures such as knee and hip replacements and heart bypass surgeries.

Of these five locations, two sites are targeting cardiovascular services, one is targeting orthopedic services, and two others are targeting both cardiovascular and orthopedic services. They are at various stages of the project.

Under this demonstration project, one single payment was negotiated for the combined services of the hospital and the physician. This bundling proposal is seen as a cost savings mechanism for Medicare. It is also an attempt to ensure hospital and physician incentives are aligned in an effort to move the patient from the most expensive level of care in a timely manner.

The ACE project continues to enforce CMS' commitment to break down the silos in which healthcare is delivered in today's society. Implementing a single bundled payment forces the inpatient provider and the physician to work in concert with each other.

Post Acute Care Bundling Plan

A second proposal is to bundle the acute hospital payment with all post acute payments. Currently, as Medicare beneficiaries with complex health conditions and multiple comorbidities move among a hospital stay and a range of post acute care providers, Medicare makes separate payments to each venue for covered services across the entire episode of care. This methodology of payment is proposed to change.

In December 2008, the Congressional Budget Office (CBO) released one of the most controversial CBO budget options addressing Medicare's payment for post acute services. President Barack Obama's 2010 proposed budget lends further support in favor of this proposal. On April 29, 2009, the Senate Finance Committee released its own version of this proposal in its Description of Policy Options entitled, "Transforming the Healthcare Delivery System: Proposals to Improve Patient Care and Reduce Health-care Costs."

The controversial solution proposed by the CBO and Senate Finance Committee and supported by President Obama is to bundle payments for acute care and post acute care services provided within the first 30 days after being discharged from an acute care hospital.

The Medicare Payment Advisory Commission (MedPAC) has expressed concern that providers do not have financial incentives to coordinate across episodes of care. MedPAC also believes that providers do not properly evaluate the full spectrum of care a patient may receive. Additionally, there is a lack of accountability of providers for all care provided during the episode of care.

In its June 2008 report, MedPAC reported that 18 percent of Medicare hospital admissions result in readmissions within 30 days postdischarge, and these readmissions accounted for $15 billion in spending in 2005. According to MedPAC, approximately $12 billion of this spending may represent potentially preventable readmissions. In light of these findings, MedPAC has recommended that Medicare payments to hospitals with relatively high readmission rates for certain conditions be reduced. In this report, MedPAC also recommended that a bundled payment system be explored for an episode of care where separate payments for distinct types of providers would be eliminated.

Post Acute Care Bundling Proposal Details

Under the CBO and Senate Finance Committee proposals, short-term acute hospitals would become the gatekeeper of all post acute care. Under the post acute care bundling plan, the unit of payment for acute care provided in hospitals would be redefined and expanded to include post acute care provided both in acute care hospitals and in nonhospital settings. Hospitals would receive a single bundled payment from Medicare for such services. Post acute payments could include home health, skilled nursing, psychiatric and rehabilitation hospitals and units, and long-term care hospital services.

The new bundled payment rates would initially be equivalent to the current rate paid for each Medicare severity diagnosis-related group (MS-DRG) plus the average costs across all post acute care settings for treating patients in that MS-DRG. Hospitals would receive the full bundled payment regardless of whether a specific patient received post acute care.

Therefore, under the proposed post acute care bundling plan, Medicare would no longer make separate payments for post acute care services following an acute care inpatient hospital stay. In other words, for the first 30 days after discharge from a short-term acute care hospital, payments for acute care and post acute care services would be bundled into one single payment to the short-term acute care hospital. Thus, post acute services would be provided either directly by the hospital or by other providers under contractual arrangements with the discharging hospital.

The CBO plan proposes that bundled payments would be implemented in three phases (see Figure 2.2). Starting in October 2014 (fiscal year [FY] 2015), Phase One would be implemented and would apply to admissions for conditions that account for the top 20 percent of post acute spending. In determining which conditions to include in the bundle for Phase One, CMS would be required to include a mix of the following conditions: chronic and acute; surgical and medical; those with significant variation in readmission and post acute spending; and those with high-volume and high post acute spending.

Phase Two would be implemented in FY2017 and would apply to admissions for conditions that would account for the next 30 percent of post

2014	April–August: CMS would release proposed and final rule. FY2015: First phase would start in October and apply to first 20% of post acute spending.
2015	First phase continues.
2016	April–August: CMS would release proposed and final rule. FY2017: Second phase would start in October and apply to next 30% of post acute spending.
2017	First and second phases continue.
2018	April–August: CMS would release proposed and final rule on final phase of bundling. FY2019: Final phase would start in October and apply to remaining 50% of post acute spending.

FIGURE 2.2
Proposed timeline for implementation of post acute bundling policy. (*Source:* Senate Finance Committee.)

acute care spending. Starting in FY2019, the final phase of bundling would be implemented and would include all other conditions and MS-DRGs that account for the remaining 50 percent of post acute care spending.

Industry Reaction

On May 15, 2009, the American Academy of Physical Medicine and Rehabilitation (AAPM&R) submitted comments to Senate Finance Committee Chair Max Baucus (D-Mont.) and Committee Ranking Minority Member Charles Grassley (R-Iowa), expressing concern relative to the committee's Description of Policy Options "Transforming the Healthcare Delivery System: Proposals to Improve Patient Care and Reduce Healthcare Costs." The AAPM&R specifically addressed the issue of bundled payments for acute and post acute hospital care and said that "without any evidence-based medicine studies to prove that the concept is indeed cost effective, any bundling proposal should be examined closely, pilot-tested, and problems should be resolved prior to implementation." The academy stated that the proposals "may negatively impact patients and the quality of care."*

---

* American Academy of Physical Medicine and Rehabilitation (AAPM&R) letter to the Honorable Max Baucus, Chairman; and the Honorable Charles Grassly, Ranking Member, of the Senate Finance Committee's Delivery System Proposals and Bundled Payments for Acute and Post Acute Hospital Care, May 15, 2009.

In addition, AAPM&R made the following recommendations to the committee that must be pursued prior to the implementation of post acute care bundling:

- conduct pilot demonstrations of any proposed bundling method (acute hospital and post acute hospital control of the bundled payment) and systematically analyze the results of any acute–post acute care (PAC) bundling experiment prior to its wholesale adoption;
- complete the PAC Payment Reform Demonstration (PAC-PRD) project, analyze data from the Continuity Assessment Record and Evaluation (CARE) tool, and factor these findings into the design and assessment of bundling; and
- obtain detailed data on clinical conditions, costs, access, and outcomes for potentially affected patients and post acute care providers.*

While the economic crisis requires change in the healthcare industry, it is imperative to ensure that proposed changes do not jeopardize the quality of patient care received in the United States. Some critics of the post acute care bundling policy comment that providing a fixed payment based on a diagnosis to the short-term acute care hospital creates an inherent financial incentive for these hospitals to underserve the most severely impaired patients. Also, bundled payment might not match the costs of treatment as well as payment currently does under Medicare's prospective payment system. These considerations must be fettered out in the coming years to ensure that patient care does not suffer to save healthcare costs.

It is the opinion of this author that the present bundling proposal is fraught with ambiguity and may have a significant impact on the delivery of post acute care—in particular, physical medicine and rehabilitation. All in all, it appears we are headed down a rocky road as we struggle with the means to maintain a balance of quality of care, quality of life, accessibility, and cost efficiency/containment. This issue will not be resolved without much dialogue and compromise.

In Chapter 3, "The Watershed Years of the American Healthcare Delivery System," the key years that defined the current healthcare delivery system are discussed. Chapter 3 also addresses the status of our country's current healthcare debate.

---

* American Academy of Physical Medicine and Rehabilitation (AAPM&R) letter to the Honorable Max Baucus, Chairman; and the Honorable Charles Grassly, Ranking Member, of the Senate Finance Committee's Delivery System Proposals and Bundled Payments for Acute and Post Acute Hospital Care, May 15, 2009.

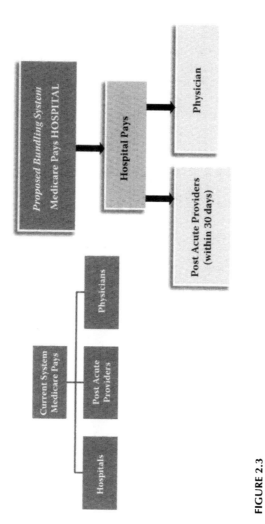

FIGURE 2.3
Transforming the healthcare delivery system bundling proposals. (*Source:* Murer Consultants, Inc.)

Reform is not an easy task, and it is unlikely the government will transform the healthcare delivery system overnight with its bundling proposal (see Figure 2.3). Regardless, the issue of appropriate use of medical resources and inpatient length of stay remains at the forefront of discussion and debate as hospitals and health systems attempt to rein in and control the cost of providing healthcare.

CHAPTER 2 ACTION ITEMS

- Understand the payment structure associated with each venue of care.
- Consider the effect CMS bundling proposal(s) could have on your facility and how you would execute and monitor this change in government payment structure.

3

The Watershed Years of the American Healthcare Delivery System

THE WATERSHED YEARS

There have been several pivotal years for healthcare in our country (see Figure 3.1). Throughout our history there have been the watershed years: 1965, 1982, and 1997.

The first watershed year was in 1965 with the introduction of Medicare. From 1965 to 1982 the government paid hospitals whatever it cost to provide care. If one case of appendicitis resulted in a three-day hospital stay costing $5,600, then Medicare paid it. If an appendicitis at another hospital on the other side of town that same day resulted in a seven-day stay and cost $15,000, Medicare paid it. It didn't matter the cost—Medicare paid the bill.

FIGURE 3.1
The watershed years.

The second watershed year came in 1982 when Congress said "no more" and implemented the diagnosis-related group (DRG) system. Under this system, the government said, for example, "We will pay $5,000 for appendicitis." It did not matter what it cost the facility or how long the patient stayed. Ultimately the government was paying the provider one payment for the hospital stay. The DRG is considered the full payment for the hospital stay, regardless of the actual number of days the patient stays in the short-term acute care hospital.

The third watershed year came in 1997 with the Balanced Budget Act (BBA). The BBA redefined the American public policy as to the sites of care delivery.

The focus turned from delivering all care in the short-term acute hospital setting to post acute care, moving the patient out of the short-term acute hospital to multivenue post acute models.

Congress, with the implementation of the BBA, put in place the *hub and spoke model* (see Figure 3.2). This model created a seamless continuum from the most costly venue of acute care to less acute and less costly levels of post acute care.

Although the focus since 1997 has been to move the patient from the acute setting (the hub) to a less intensive, less costly setting, there continues to be a reluctance by some to move the patient appropriately through the healthcare continuum.

In March 2010, President Barack Obama signed the Patient Protection and Affordable Care Act, which changes access to care and the future of the health delivery system.

THE BARRIER DEFINED

There is something wrong when, on a Monday, a patient is on day five in the intensive care unit and on Tuesday morning is discharged home. When Congress implemented the hub and spoke model, its intention was to get the patient out of the most expensive venue, the hub (acute care), and into the spokes (post acute venues of care).

Other countries have different models of healthcare delivery. For example, in Germany, most rehabilitation is performed in an inpatient setting with very little outpatient rehabilitation. Yet in the United States, there is a push

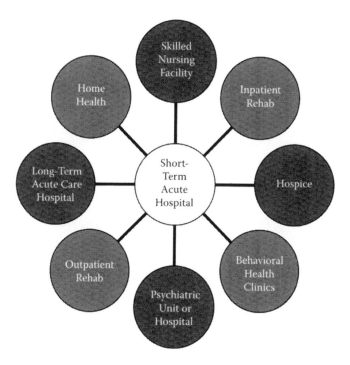

FIGURE 3.2

The American healthcare delivery system: the hub and spoke model. (*Source:* Murer Consultants, Inc.)

to get the patient out of the most expensive inpatient level of care and provide as much at the post acute setting as possible.

Although everyone would like their patients to remain in the hub for their entire stay, as good stewards, it's everyone's responsibility to focus on moving the patient from the most expensive venue to less costly and less restrictive post acute venues of care.

One might ask: Is one approach to healthcare better or worse than the other? Is one way the right way and another the wrong way? Not necessarily. They are all different approaches in the way healthcare is provided. In the United States, the policy is to move the patient along the continuum, ensuring he or she is in the right place at the right time for the right reimbursement and the right utilization of resources

Elderly patients, especially those with early signs of dementia, have a tendency to become depressed, and their mental status can deteriorate when they have prolonged inpatient stays.

Muscles weaken, pressure sores can develop, and blood clots can form from lying idle in the bed. Infections can be contracted. Little movement can increase the risk of falling when people get up and are dizzy or light-headed. All these conditions support the need for patients to stay in a hospital setting for as few days as possible.

Furthermore, in some cases, hospitals can make you sick. MRSA (methicillin-resistant *Staphylococcus aureus*) and other infections can be acquired in the hospital setting. To stem this issue, Section 1886 (d)(4) (D) of the Social Security Act now requires acute hospitals to report when certain diagnoses are present on admission to the hospital. Hospitals are penalized with lower payments when specific diagnoses are acquired in the hospital.

In addition, medical errors do occur. For example, the wrong medication or the wrong dosage could be administered. These adverse events that cause harm to a patient as a result of medical error are also being reviewed, and certain "never events" (events that should never occur in a healthcare setting) are no longer being paid for by Medicare.

In most cases, the facility is financially better off with shorter lengths of stay. As explained previously, Medicare pays the hospital a predetermined amount, and the hospital is not paid for additional days unless the patient's extended stay triggers a high cost outlier.

High cost outliers are paid to hospitals and some post acute venues that incur extraordinary cost associated with providing care to individuals. However, the cost has to exceed a predetermined threshold amount, and then only a percentage of the actual cost is reimbursed. Details of reimbursement, including high cost outlier reimbursements, are discussed further in Chapter 6.

HEALTHCARE REFORM: 2010—A MAJOR WATERSHED YEAR

Many policy ideas have surfaced as part of plans to restructure America's healthcare delivery system. With healthcare spending in 2009 accounting for nearly 17 percent of the nation's gross domestic product (GDP) and projections that it will account for 21 percent of the GDP by 2020, it is more important than ever to move the patient from the most expensive venue, acute care, to a less expensive venue, post acute care (see Figure 3.3).

FIGURE 3.3
2010 healthcare reform?

In the March 2009 White House Forum on Health Reform, President Obama called the ever-growing cost of healthcare "one of the greatest threats to Americans' well-being and economic success." The Obama Administration has been focusing on two options:

- A public health insurance (in addition to Medicare and Medicaid)
- Private health insurance

The pros to these options are that they could significantly control healthcare costs. The cons come in the form of more government control. Much of the debate regarding healthcare reform centers on the feasibility of a public health insurance plan option. The private insurance industry is vehemently opposed to this option. There was public discourse as issues related to socialized medicine and government-mandated euthanasia surfaced in false claims and scare tactics.

No matter the outcome of this debate, for healthcare reform to be effective, case management must be a part of a truly integrated health system. All the players—hospitals, post acute venues and physicians—must operate under the same incentives. One sector cannot benefit when the same incentive penalizes the other. Optimizing use of all resources for the primary purpose of ensuring strength and availability of the health system in perpetuity is everyone's fiduciary responsibility.

One of our greatest challenges in healthcare today is the continued lack of consistency in healthcare regulations. The Centers for Medicare and Medicaid Services (CMS) continues to change their regulations on an increasingly faster pace, which interferes with institutions' long-term vision and financial planning. It makes it difficult for those participating in the healthcare delivery system to plan for the future if regulations keep changing.

The future must have clearly defined regulations. The principal basis of healthcare delivery must be reconfirmed: a privilege for the few, or a basic right for all citizens? The debate continues to rage. The payment structure must also be defined. Will there be multiple payments or one comprehensive payment, and what will be included in these payments? All these questions must be answered if true healthcare reform is to take place.

Will 2010 be our country's next watershed year? This will depend upon policymakers effectively and comprehensively defining healthcare policy. Is the American healthcare delivery system truly broken, or is it simply in need of adjustment in the context of today's society?

In the context of day-to-day hospital management, however, it is more important than ever to identify key obstacles in reducing the length of stay. Once these obstacles are identified, a plan to reduce or eliminate them can be put in place. This will allow the patient to move to the right venue in the timeliest manner.

The next chapter focuses on the most repeated obstacles in reducing length of stay. Although one of the keys to reducing length of stay continues to be the dichotomy between payment to the hospital and payment to the physician, there are other contributing factors. Chapter 4 identifies key obstacles in the fight to reduce the patient's average length of stay.

CHAPTER 3 ACTION ITEMS

- What were the key watershed years, and how did they affect our nation's healthcare delivery system?
- Does your facility operate within a complete hub and spoke model?

4

Key Obstacles in Reducing Length of Stay

CAJOLING CAN NO LONGER BE THE PRIMARY METHODOLOGY FOR DEALING WITH PHYSICIANS

Each time the concept of "cajoling" is presented during a group session with case managers, the participants respond with a resounding round of applause. Webster's dictionary defines *cajole* as "to persuade with flattery or gentle urging especially in the face of reluctance. To coax."

Should flattering or coaxing a physician into moving a patient to a more appropriate venue, based on medical needs and necessity, be the primary tool of case management? Just because Dr. Carter has worked with Nurse Frost for more than 15 years and will listen to what she says is by no means an effective way to ensure throughput of patients along the continuum. Everyone needs to become good stewards of the resources of the health system and move the patient when it is appropriate—not because of persuasiveness, but because it is the right thing to do.

THE LARGEST OBSTACLE

Physicians are typically thought to be the largest barrier in moving the patient through the healthcare system. Every hospital has a group of physicians who are known for keeping their patients too long. How often have you heard a case manager say, "I cringe when I know Dr. Christian is the attending. I know our length of stay will increase and that a timely discharge will be difficult."

Physicians offer a number of reasons for not wanting to move the patient. "We'll talk about it tomorrow;" "I said so;" "I'm not comfortable moving the patient." These excuses all contribute to not moving the patient and add days to the patient's acute length of stay.

Physicians' rounding in the evening can delay a discharge until the following morning when the patient could have discharged the previous day had the doctor rounded earlier. Families can manipulate the physician by pleading, "Please, Doc, can't Mom stay one more day?" All these issues result in an increase in the length of stay for which there is no additional payment and case management has little effect.

CULTURAL CHANGE

To make any significant behavioral changes, health systems must experience cultural change. The chief medical officer or chief of staff must enforce the hospital's stance in moving patients along the continuum. There needs to be a recalibration of the physician's internal code of ethics and an acceptable level of peer culture.

The health system can no longer afford the rhetoric of "We have always done it that way" or "It's my patient and I'll move him when I'm ready." In today's world, hospitals will no longer be financially viable if these practices continue. Additional days can add up to millions of dollars in uncompensated care. The chief medical officer, with support from administration, must provide the direction and oversight to ensure that the entire case management team works together in an effort to reduce the health system's length of stay, which ultimately affects the cost of providing care.

SOCIAL ISSUES

Social issues also play a role in patient length of stay. Patients may be admitted through the emergency department with little or no medical complexities except for the fact that they cannot take care of themselves. It is questionable whether or why they should have been admitted in the first place, yet without family support the patients cannot be sent home and are admitted. The physician is frustrated and feels his hands are tied. The patient was admitted through the ER; therefore, the attending physician or hospitalist—and ultimately the hospital—is responsible for the care of this patient. However, the financial impact ends there. The physician bills and is paid, regardless of the patient's length of stay. The hospital bills, but will only be compensated based on the diagnosis-related group (DRG) assigned. Additionally, if it is subsequently determined the patient did not meet medical necessity, the hospital payment can be denied.

PREFERENCE FOR THE INTENSIVE CARE UNIT

Most physicians would love to have all ICU beds. They are comfortable with the nursing staff and believe patients receive better care in the ICU. Well, of course the physicians prefer these units. The ICU nurses do tend to spoil the physicians, and generally these nurses are the most experienced in the hospital. They call the physician less often, and because it's the ICU, provide more direct patient care. That's just it. It is an intensive care unit designed to allow for a heightened level of care during medical crisis. But this service comes at a price. It's the most expensive unit in the hospital. The health system will need the cooperation of administration and the ICU medical directors to ensure that physicians move their patients to the next venue in a timely manner.

CONSULTING PHYSICIAN

In some instances, the patient may have four or five consulting specialty physicians involved in his or her care. The behavior of this group of physicians implies there must be a committee decision to move the patient to the next level of care. Two physicians might agree to moving or discharging the patient on Tuesday, but if the other three physicians can't be tracked down the patient stays until Wednesday, thereby adding an additional day to the length of stay in an acute care bed.

ATTENDING PHYSICIAN IN THE ROLE OF QUARTERBACK

In today's health system it is common for the attending physician to utilize the services of consulting physicians. In some instances, there seems to be an overutilization of consulting physicians. With so many physicians involved in a case, the tendency is for no single physician to oversee the care of the patient and ensure that the patient is moving appropriately through the health system.

If the attending physician truly embraced the role of the quarterback, he or she would ensure that the patient is moved efficiently and appropriately through the continuum. This would reduce delays waiting for a consensus among the physicians involved in the case. This is not to say the consulting physician's opinion is not important, but it is to stress the importance of the quarterback overseeing the process and taking the responsibility of ensuring the patient does not remain in an acute setting unnecessarily.

Having several consulting physicians on a case can cause a delay in moving the patient appropriately. Therefore, it is critical that the attending physician, in the style of a quarterback, be responsible for the timely discharge or transfer of the patient. It should be the attending physician's responsibility to contact and get the consensus of the consulting physician, and ultimately to ensure that the patient is moved to the next level of care in a timely manner.

HOW TO DEAL WITH A DIFFICULT PHYSICIAN

Some physicians become passive-aggressive when approached by a nurse or case manager about moving their patient. In fact, some physicians may keep the patient even longer just to prove a point. Again, communication is key.

However, don't have the *conversation in your head*. It is important to communicate directly with the physician.

Ask the physician to explain his or her concerns in moving the patient to the next level of care. Jot it down and report it to your supervisor, and remember your ABCs and D:

- Acknowledge their concern.
- Be respectful and listen.
- Communicate these concerns to your supervisor.
- Don't be confrontational.

The physician must ensure that documentation in the chart supports medical necessity to warrant keeping the patient in this unit or venue. There has to be strong medical leadership to ensure the medical staff will move their patients appropriately. The case management staff needs to be confident that a medical director will take action. There is nothing worse than when the case management staff gives up, citing, "Even when we report a problem, our supervisors do nothing about it. No one wants to upset the physician."

OTHER OBSTACLES

Of course there are other obstacles besides the physician that contribute to extending the patient's length of stay. Each facility has its own set of special circumstances that can lead to a patient staying too long in the short-term acute care hospital. The key is to identify the obstacles at your facility and develop a plan to eliminate or minimize the issues that negatively affect the length of stay.

Obstacle: Physical Plant

The majority of hospitals today are moving away from semiprivate rooms. A July 2006 article in *USA Today* quoted industry experts as stating that any rooms added in the future will need to be private to comply with new guidelines followed by most states. The article also stated there was a growing body of evidence showing private rooms pay for themselves by reducing infection rates, reducing recovery time, and making patient care more efficient. Private rooms versus semiprivate rooms can also affect the length of stay. For example:

- Limited Private Rooms: The length of stay can increase when a patient doesn't want to leave the privacy of his or her own room in the short-term acute care hospital to be treated in a skilled nursing unit that offers semiprivate rooms. When Medicare or the private insurance carrier is responsible for payment, the patient should not be allowed to dictate where he or she prefers to receive treatment. If the patient ultimately refuses to move on to the next level of care based on room choice, it is important to explain to the patient that the only other option is to discharge home. Staying in the acute bed to avoid a semiprivate skilled room should not be an option. The patient should not be allowed to remain in the acute bed simply because he or she does not want to share a semiprivate room.

- Semiprivate Rooms: Another negative impact of semiprivate rooms is "bed block" based on infection or gender. A 20-bed unit with semiprivate rooms can have limited beds available at any given time due to these factors. This causes the patient to remain in the acute bed until an appropriate room at the post acute venue becomes available, adding to the patient's length of stay in the acute hospital.

Obstacle: Monitoring Equipment

Many physicians have a preference to have all their patients in a monitored bed. These physicians will keep the patient in a telemetry unit if a monitored bed is not available on the medical or surgical floor. When this happens, a patient truly in need of a monitored bed will sit another day in an ICU because telemetry beds are full with patients who no longer need constant monitoring.

Obstacle: We Wait and Wait for Approval

There are physicians whose operant is a "decide as you go" attitude with no treatment plans or orders in place. This can cause delays in moving the patient appropriately. Additionally, some managed care or commercial payers can take two or three days to return calls to the case managers or social workers regarding a discharge. These obstacles can increase the length of stay.

Obstacle: Staffing Shortage

We are all aware of the nursing shortage in the healthcare industry. Many times when a nurse calls in sick, there is no replacement. Even health systems with an in-house nursing agency can't fill all vacancies including weekend coverage and call-offs, and many facilities won't use outside agencies. When there are not enough nurses for these post acute venues, the patient remains in the acute bed unnecessarily.

Physical plant, equipment, and staffing issues all can affect the overall length of stay. Unfortunately, not every obstacle can be eliminated. It is unlikely that all physical plant issues like semiprivate rooms can be eliminated. However, these issues should be closely monitored to ensure that the patient is moved as quickly as possible when an appropriate bed becomes available. The case management team must strive to reduce or eliminate as many of these roadblocks as possible to move the patient in the timeliest manner.

IS THE POST ACUTE VENUE READY?

There is nothing more frustrating than for the case management team to have all their ducks in a row and yet the patient stays in the acute bed another day. The patient is ready, all the forms have been filled out, the insurance company has approved the next level of care, and yet the post acute venue informs you it cannot accept the patient at this time.

There is no legitimate reason for the delay. There are plenty of beds, but the patient is not accepted due to some hidden rule. The patient sits another day in the short-term acute hospital waiting to be transferred until after a shift change or because "it's getting late—let's wait until tomorrow."

There are all kinds of reasons for the delay: "Everyone knows the skilled nursing unit won't take a patient after 3:00 p.m." "It's Friday and home health is short-handed this weekend, so they won't be able to see the patient until Monday." "The physiatrist at the rehab hospital has clinic hours beginning at 2:00 p.m. each afternoon, so if you want your patient admitted, you'd better have them there before noon or they will have to wait until the next day." The list goes on and on.

A hospital may be physically open seven days per week, 24 hours per day, but operationally it's a five-day workweek. There is generally little movement of patients on the weekend. There is limited lab, radiology, and other key ancillary services available. These are all obstructions that contribute to an increase in the length of stay of the patient.

These scenarios are prevalent at many healthcare institutions. Every facility has a *secret underground* by which it operates. Although there are no official policies or procedures to warrant this behavior, nevertheless, it's the unwritten rule.

SLOW DOWN, YOU'RE MOVING TOO FAST

Timeliness of moving the patient to the next level of care when medically appropriate is essential. However, sometimes hospitals and health systems get so caught up in their financial bottom line that they assume the only way to reduce cost is to move the patient out of the short-term acute bed.

Hospital chief executive officers across the country are calling for half-day or full-day reductions in the average length of stay. They see a decrease in the length of stay as the magic bullet that will solve their financial woes.

At some point, health systems must determine the driving force for moving these patients out. There comes a time when hospitals need to step back and ask themselves what an appropriate length of stay is for their institution. If they are the only tertiary facility in the area and are responsible for the most difficult cases, they should expect a higher average length of stay. Perhaps the hospital is located in an area that has been hit hard with the current economic downturn. Or perhaps the community they serve has an expectation of a longer length of stay. No matter the reason, some hospitals will experience longer lengths of stay.

Of course, keeping patients too long in a venue that is no longer appropriate is a waste of money, but pushing patients out the door before they are medically ready creates a host of new problems.

For example, an elderly gentleman is sent home after an above-the-knee amputation. At discharge, he and his wife are given instructions on how to care for the wound and instructed to follow up with his primary care physician. Unfortunately, the couple does not follow these instructions, the wound becomes infected, and within days he ends up presenting to the emergency room with a high fever and a rampant infection. Was he sent home too soon? It's hard to say, but this happens every day, and one has to ask if a few more days in acute care would have prevented this scenario.

Continually trying to reduce the length of stay is a delicate balancing act, and sending patients home too early can backfire if this trend begins to cause an increase in the number of patients being readmitted to the hospital. Hospitals must agree on a target average length of stay based on the patients they treat and the diagnostic mix of the population they serve.

A number of Medicare patients each year return to the hospital within days or weeks after discharge. This trend has resulted in the government targeting readmissions to the hospital. These readmissions are costly, and the government believes reducing them could save precious healthcare dollars.

The Medicare Payment Advisory Commission (MedPAC) reported in its June 2008 report that 18 percent of Medicare hospital admissions resulted in readmissions within 30 days post-discharge. Readmissions account for billions of dollars in spending. MedPAC has recommended that Medicare payments to hospitals with relatively high readmission rates for certain conditions be reduced.

In April 2009, the Senate Finance Committee issued a report with policy options to transform the American Healthcare Delivery System. One proposal takes steps to reduce avoidable and preventable hospital readmissions. It establishes payment incentives to improve patient care and encourage greater care coordination among acute and post acute providers. It also proposes to reduce payments to hospitals with relatively high readmissions for select conditions. These proposals, as with the current payment structure, do not equally apply to the physician and the hospital. The problem continues to be the lack of incentives to physicians in moving the patient through the continuum of care.

There continues to be a misalignment in the delivery of healthcare dollars in our country. Until all participants are on the same playing field, there will continue to be little cooperation among the parties. Therefore, the opportunity lies in the effective use of the post acute venues of care. These opportunities are discussed in Chapter 5.

CHAPTER 4 ACTION ITEMS

- Identify your key obstacles in reducing length of stay.
- What obstacles can be eliminated or minimized? Are there some obstacles that cannot be changed?
- Does your institution have a policy for dealing with difficult physicians?

5

Opportunities for Effective
Use of Post Acute Venues

VENUE MANAGEMENT

How do you decide on the appropriate venue for a patient needing further medical attention? The first step is knowing your *post acute menu*. You need to identify your options and determine what is available in your health system as well as your community.

What items/venues are on your menu?

- Long-Term Acute Care Hospital
- Inpatient Rehabilitation
- Skilled Nursing Facility
- Outpatient Rehabilitation
- Home Health
- Hospice

The second step is distinguishing among and between venue options. Every member of the case management team must become an expert in the intended distinction of the care delivery sites and be versatile as to the capabilities and outcome expectations of each venue of care.

The most judicious method of applying a multiuse continuum strategy is by using discharge triggers from the most restrictive environment as the admission criteria of the lesser restrictive venue.

A centralized system of case management ensures frugal utilization of the most expensive inpatient acute services and enhanced utilization of reasonable, appropriate, less costly alternative delivery sites such as skilled care, home health, and outpatient therapy.

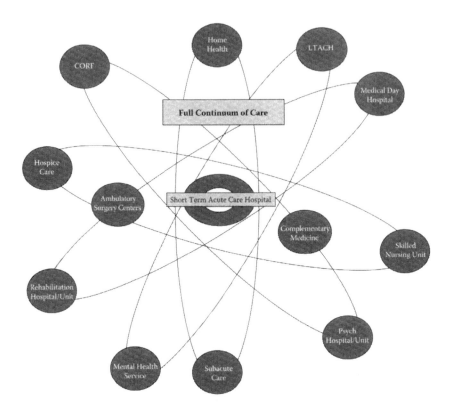

FIGURE 5.1
Full continuum of care. (*Source:* Murer Consultants, Inc.)

Each post acute venue of care is designed for a specific patient population. At the end of a patient's inpatient stay it is important that the patient discharge to the most appropriate venue of care.

The most successful case management depends on the availability of multiple and diverse venues of care. A full continuum of care (Figure 5.1) can mitigate the revenue loss of patients staying beyond the diagnosis-related group (DRG) length of stay in the short-term acute care hospital. Post acute venues afford the short-term acute care hospital the opportunity to capture additional revenue by turning over the acute bed.

CENTRALIZED CASE MANAGEMENT SYSTEM

Centralized case management is emerging as the necessary link in the chain that holds together the integrated healthcare delivery system. As integrated delivery systems are formed by parties with varying incentives and areas of expertise, it becomes even more critical to bridge these differences through case management. To be successful, the case management system must address the agendas of multiple and diverse audiences.

A case management system should be designed in a horizontal fashion. Case management should be contacted once a patient is identified as needing post acute services. The centralized case management department will determine the best venue to place the patient based on the patient's medical needs.

A strong, well-organized, centralized case management system is a key component for optimal operation of a full continuum of care. Case management is a system designed to identify, coordinate, and direct all services utilized in the delivery of healthcare. The goal of case management is to place the patient in the right venue of care at the right time based on the patient's medical needs.

In an integrated healthcare system, case management should be centralized so that all of the case managers throughout the system, including the various hospitals and post acute venues, are utilizing the same system policies and procedures for patient case management. A successful case management system must have case managers at a common level of knowledge regarding care options, venue options, clinical goals, anticipated outcomes, and the regulatory and compliance implications involved with the various venues of care.

Occasionally a case manager will run into a physician who is not with the program and believes that physicians do not have to concern themselves with the length of stay. Dr. Smith is from the old school and believes the patient is paying for the stay and therefore the patient can stay as long as he or she wants. Dr. Smith pays no attention to things like DRG lengths of stay or Medicare days.

When this happens it is imperative that case management has strong administrative support backing them up and will support any further action needed to be taken against a problem physician. When administration offers no support, a number of physicians will continue this behavior, given that there are no negative consequences.

The cost savings of a truly integrated case management system is realized when the case manager is able to move the patient appropriately along the continuum of care from the costly acute setting to a less costly outpatient setting.

Under this approach, case managers and other key individuals should be educated to ensure each has a broad knowledge of the specialized treatment each post acute venue offers, whether it is a long-term acute care hospital, the comprehensive inpatient rehabilitation unit, skilled nursing, or outpatient.

Case management is the primary tool to effectively serve patients with numerous and complex needs while simultaneously seeking to reduce utilization and costs. Increased competition, consolidation, and maturity of the healthcare industry, compounded by regulatory changes, challenge health systems to continue to be self-reflective and examine their position within the markets they serve. The health system must examine its existing venues and determine where the patient can best receive the most appropriate level of care while keeping in mind the overall financial performance of the health system.

The case manager must become expert in the intended distinctions between each care delivery venue and pose the hard questions about the capabilities and outcome expectations for those providers who function within each venue. Figure 5.2 is an overview of each of these key venues. Each individual venue has a specific expectation including the following:

- Payment structure
- Direct nursing hours per patient day
- Physician coverage
- Anticipated patient condition
- Patient stability
- Anticipated average length of stay
- Average payment

Each post acute venue has a role in the continuum of care, which is examined in the following chapter. Chapter 6 provides an overview of the post acute venues of care, including those of the long-term acute care hospital, the comprehensive inpatient rehabilitation hospital, the skilled nursing unit, and outpatient, including home health and hospice.

CHAPTER 5 ACTION ITEMS

- What post acute venues are available in your continuum and community?
- What are the key elements that distinguish each post acute venue?

	ICU	Acute Hospital	Critical Access Hospital	Long-Term Acute Care Hospital	Rehab Unit	Skilled/Subacute	Outpatient/CORF
Type of Facility	Generally a unit of a short-term hospital	Short-term acute care hospital	State designated; no more than 25 beds including swing beds; located approx. 35+ miles from other facilities	Freestanding or hospital within a hospital	Unit or hospital	Unit or facility	Outpatient services
Payment Structure	Prospective payment system under DRGs	PPS under DRGs	Cost based	PPS exempt under LTC-DRGs	PPS exempt under case mix groups	PPS exempt under MDS/RUG categories	CPT codes
Direct Nursing Hours per Patient Day	Average 19 hours	Average 7.25 to 8 hours	RN, CNA, or LPN on duty when there are patients in facility	Average 8.5	Average 5.5	Average 4	Average 1.5
Physician	Daily or more with specialist contact	Daily	At least one available within 30 minutes	Daily	Daily, average 5 days per week	Intermittent, average 3 days per week	Intermittent less than 1 day per week
Condition	May change by the minute	May change by the day	ER or short-term stay	May change by the week or day	May change by the week	May change by the week	Medically stable
Stability	Patient in crisis	Possibility for crisis	Possibility for crisis	Possibility for crisis	Newly stable	Newly stable	Medically stable
Average Length of Stay	1–5 days	3–5 days	96 hours	18–35 days	10–22 days	7–20 days	2–10 weeks
Average Payment	$1,800 per diem	$1,200 per diem	$2,500 per discharge	$1,300 per diem	$650 per diem	$300 per diem	$3,000 per discharge

Notes: CORF = comprehensive outpatient rehabilitation facility, PPS = prospective payment system, DRG = diagnosis-related group, LTC-DRG = long-term care diagnosis-related group, MDS = minimum data set, RUG = resource utilization group, CPT = current procedural terminology, RN = registered nurse, CNA = certified nurse assistant, LPN = licensed practical nurse, ER = emergency room.

FIGURE 5.2

Overview—key venues of care. (*Source:* Murer Consultants, Inc.)

6

Post Acute Venues and Their Roles in the Continuum

INTRODUCTION: POST ACUTE VENUES

As Americans age, they require more complex medical services such as advanced treatment for heart disease, stroke, and other chronic aliments. With Americans living longer and longer, there is an ever-growing need for post acute venues of care.

Over the past decade, Centers for Medicare and Medicaid Services (CMS) has reviewed rules and regulations concerning key post acute care venues on an annual basis. These reviews are CMS' attempt to rightly size the continuum of care.

Patients need to move along the post acute continuum of care once their short-term acute hospital stay is over. It is important for a health system to have available the means for treating these patients who no longer need short-term acute care but have conditions and comorbidities that prohibit discharging them home. These post acute venues should not compete but should complement one another.

For example, a patient presents to the emergency department with a stroke. The patient is stablized and spends several days in the short-term acute hospital setting. The physician determines the patient needs additional therapy services. Depending on the condition and needs of the patient, he or she could qualify for several different venues of care: inpatient rehabilitation facility (IRF), long-term acute care hospital (LTACH), skilled nursing unit (SNU), home with home healthcare, or outpatient therapy.

Because the patient falls under a rehabilitation diagnostic category, if the patient can tolerate three hours of therapy per day, this patient should discharge to a rehabilitation hospital/unit. However, if the patient has a number of comorbidites and cannot tolerate the intense therapy provided in an inpatient rehab program but has high nursing needs, the patient may be appropriate for an LTACH.

On the other hand, if the patient is less acute and has minimal nursing needs that can be treated with approximately 4–5 hours of nursing each day with minimal contact with a physician, then perhaps a skilled unit may be able to address the patient's needs. Finally, if the patient has no acute needs but still needs additional treatment, it may be appropriate to discharge the patient home with home healthcare or home with outpatient therapy.

This patient could use one or several of the post acute venues available: discharge from acute to an LTACH to inpatient rehabilitation; discharge from acute to inpatient rehabilitation to skilled; or even discharge from the LTACH to skilled. It depends on the needs of the individual patient as well as the post acute venues available within the community.

In many instances, if a specific post acute venue is not available within the continuum, those that are available will compensate for the missing piece. For example, if there is no LTACH, the patient may be sent inappropriately to a skilled unit even though a skilled unit is not designed or compensated appropriately to treat a patient with a high-acuity condition.

It is important to note that an LTACH is not a replacement for skilled nursing or rehab and vice versa. Each of these venues should have specific admission criteria and discharge protocols. Each venue has a clear definition of purpose and scope of service to be provided to the patient. Once the patient no longer meets criteria for the specific level of care, case management must facilitate movement to the next venue including discharge home. Everyone on the case management team plays an important role in ensuring that the right patient is in the right post acute venue for the right reimbursement.

The following sections provide an overview of key post acute venues of care. Each section provides criteria for the venue and a brief description of the Medicare payment structure associated with it.

LONG-TERM ACUTE CARE HOSPITAL

Overview

LTACHs have been an integral part of the continuum of care since the early 1980s. However, with all the changes, regulatory updates, and three-year moratorium for any new LTACH, satellite, or increase in beds (the moratorium was set to expire at the end of 2010, but was extended for an additional two years until 2012 under the March 2010 health reform bill), LTACHs are an essential part of the continuum of care.

There are approximately 400 LTACHs in the United States today, treating 130,000 patients each year. An LTACH patient is inappropriate for a short-term acute care hospital. The inpatient prospective payment system (IPPS) does not sufficiently cover costs of an extended stay patient with acute hospital needs.

In fact, Congress created LTACHs to care for the small patient population of extremely ill patients for whom the cost of care is beyond the scope of what the majority of short-term acute care hospitals should provide based on the short-term payment. LTACHs serve a valuable role in the continuum of care by caring for the critically ill patient who requires a longer stay than the typical short-term inpatient stay.

Patients who remain in the short-term hospital beyond five to seven days generally begin to accumulate uncompensated care. There is no payment for these additional days. The short-term acute care hospital is also financially affected in that it cannot turn over the bed to allow for additional payment.

For systems without an LTACH, the patient can remain in the short-term acute care hospital far longer than the expected length of stay. Or as an alternative, the patient can be transferred to a skilled nursing unit, which is ill-equipped both financially and clinically to care for these patients with high-acuity needs.

LTACHs are essential to an effective continuum of care as a key venue within a health system. LTACHs should be the mirror image of the referring short-term acute care hospital serving those patients whose medical conditions require a stay longer than the CMS-prescribed diagnosis-related group (DRG).

Regulatory

LTACHs must meet the Medicare Part 482 Conditions of Participation for Hospitals. These regulations provide the requirements for hospital operations under the Medicare program such as administration, basic hospital functions, and requirements for specialty hospitals.

LTACHs must be licensed by the state in which they intend to operate and are typically licensed as general or specialty acute care hospital beds. They are not licensed as nursing homes or intermediate care facilities.

TABLE 6.1

CMS' Support for Long Term Acute Care Hospitals:
Comparison Proposed & Final Rate Adjustments

Rate Year	Base Rate	High Cost Outlier Fixed Loss Amount
• FY 2003—Proposed	$27,649	$29,852
RY 2003—FINAL	**$34,956**	**$24,450**
• RY 2004—Proposed	$35,726	$19,978
RY 2004—FINAL	**$35,726**	**$19,590**
• RY 2005—Proposed	$36,762	$21,864
RY 2005—FINAL	**$36,833**	**$17,864**
• FY 2006—Proposed	$37,975	$11,544
RY 2006—FINAL	**$38,086**	**$10,501**
• RY 2007—Proposed	$38,086	$18,489
RY 2007—FINAL	**$38,086**	**$14,887**
• RY 2008—Proposed	$38,356	$18,774
RY 2008—FINAL	**$38,356**	**$20,738**
RY 2009—FINAL	**$39,114**	**$22,960**
RY 2010—FINAL	**$39,896**	**$18,425**
• RY 2010— Revised	$39,795	$18,615
RY 2011—FINAL	**$39,599**	**$18,785**

Source: Chart by Murer Consultants.

Just like patients in a short-term acute care hospital, patients in an LTACH must have the medical necessity requiring an acute level of inpatient care. Once a patient no longer meets these criteria, discharge planning should move the patient to the next appropriate level of care, which could include discharge to home or to another post acute venue.

Over the past decade, CMS has reviewed rules and regulations concerning key post acute care venues on an annual basis. These reviews are CMS' attempt to right-size the continuum of care. Each year there continues to be a positive impact to LTACHs. The base rate has increased from $34,956 in rate year (RY) 2003 to $39,896 in RY2010. The high cost outlier threshold has fluctuated over the years from a high of $24,450 in RY2003 to a low of $10,501 in 2006 (see Table 6.1).

Generally, CMS publishes its new rules for LTACHs in late summer. The 2011 Final Rules for LTACH were made available on Friday, July 30, 2010. These new rules go into effect each October. The 2011 base rate for LTACHs was set at $39,599 and the threshold amount $18,785.

Congress has continued to see the value of this unique post acute venue of care. The LTACH offers a vehicle for cost-efficient interface of healthcare programs offered by various community providers. Furthermore, the LTACH completes the circle of venue options as the conduit between general acute care and community skilled care.

Length of Stay

It is important to remember an LTACH is an acute care hospital. The only difference is the Medicare aggregate length of stay (at year end) must be at least 25 days. Not all patients will have a length of stay of 25 days. Some patients can have an outside range of 14–45 days, but the target range is typically 18–35 days (Figure 6.1).

LTACHs are designed to treat medically complex patients. They are not nursing homes or palliative care centers (Figure 6.2). They are acute hospitals for critical care, and some can be comparable to ICUs or CCUs. In fact, many LTACHs will have designated beds that act as an ICU and have even higher staff-to-patient ratios within the LTACH. These patients have the medical necessity to require an intense acute level of care. The design of LTACHs and the staffing are based on treating these high-acuity patients and, therefore, there should be limited transfers back to the short-term acute care hospital (Figure 6.3).

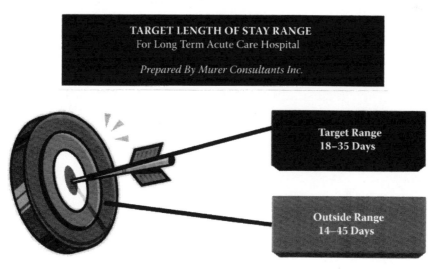

TARGET LENGTH OF STAY RANGE
For Long Term Acute Care Hospital

Prepared By Murer Consultants Inc.

**Target Range
18–35 Days**

**Outside Range
14–45 Days**

FIGURE 6.1
Target length of stay range for long-term acute care hospital.

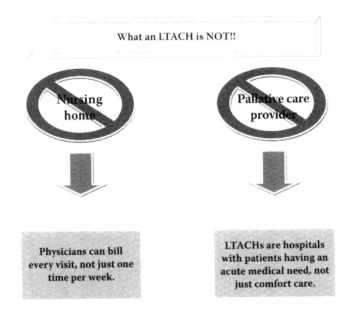

FIGURE 6.2
What a long-term acute care hospital is not.

Benefits and Conditions

Some of the benefits of an LTACH include the following:

- Extending the continuum of care
- Diminishing (short-term acute hospital) DRG revenue loss
- Recognition by managed care payment structure
- No limitation on type of diagnoses
- No limitation on age
- No limitation on scope of services provided
- Ability to cross-utilize services and resources within the health system continuum

There are many conditions appropriate for LTACH care and reimbursement including the following:

- Medically complex
- Respiratory disorders including tracheostomy
- Ventilator dependent
- Cardiac/cardiovascular conditions
- Renal disease
- Oncology

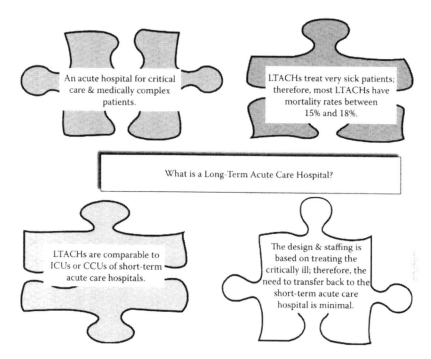

FIGURE 6.3
What is a long-term acute care hospital?

- Wound care (wound management should be secondary to a primary diagnosis appropriate for admission)
- Reconstructive and extended postsurgical care
- Rehabilitation-related diagnoses with complex or tertiary needs

Physician Coverage

LTACHs operate under an open staff model. The physician follows his or her patients and sees them on a daily basis, just like in a short-term acute care hospital. If the physician chooses not to follow the patients, the LTACH's medical director, or in some cases a hospitalist, is available.

Reimbursement for physician services in an LTACH is identical to that of a short-term acute care hospital. The physician bills under Part B for Medicare patients or submits bills for commercial or managed care payers, in the identical format that they bill the short-term acute care hospital.

All LTACHs must have their own credentialed medical staff. Any physician wishing to practice at the LTACH must undergo the credentialing process and be credentialed by the LTACH.

TABLE 6.2

DRG 193 Simple Pneumonia and Pleurisy with MCC

Short-Term Acute Care Hospital	Long-Term Acute Care Hospital
AMLOS = 6.5 (GMLOS = 5.3)	GMLOS (5/6th) = 20.9 (17.4)
Payment = $7,640	Payment = $30,175
IPPS Weight = 1.4796	LTC-DRG Weight = 0.7620

Source: CMS National Rates for 2011.
Note: AMLOS = arithmetic mean length of stay; GMLOS = geometric mean length of stay.

LTACH Payment Structure

LTACHs are paid under the DRG system. This system is identical to the IPPS payment system for short-term acute hospitals except that LTACH DRGs have different weights, which are applied to a much higher base rate. The anticipated length of stay in an LTACH is much higher than the anticipated length of stay in the short-term acute hospital to compensate for these complex patients. For an example, see Table 6.2.

An LTACH is an ideal vehicle to stem losses due to extended lengths of stay and increased patient acuity at the short-term acute care hospital. Ideally, an LTACH operates within a total healthcare system to complete the full continuum while providing a venue of care where the patient can be treated for an extended length of stay with commensurate reimbursement. LTACHs are a critical component in an effective continuum of care. The LTACH as a venue of care has made a positive impact with its effectiveness on the continuum.

The LTACH should reflect the patient diagnostic population of the referring short-term acute care hospital in harmony with the mission and philosophy of the health system and its medical staff. Together, the LTACH and the short-term acute care hospital form the continuum of care with appropriate reimbursement reflective of each venue's purpose and anticipated length of stay.

COMPREHENSIVE INPATIENT REHABILITATION HOSPITAL/UNIT

Overview

IRFs are a critical venue in the post acute continuum of care. An IRF provides specialized services to patients with functional deficits. Currently, there are more than 200 freestanding IRFs and just under 1,000 inpatient rehabilitation units in acute care hospitals. Medicare pays IRFs at a higher rate than other healthcare providers because IRFs are designed to offer specialized rehabilitation care to patients with the most intensive needs.

Identifying potential rehab candidates early in their acute stay will reduce the number of days the patient remains in the acute bed for which the hospital is no longer receiving payment.

Rehabilitation inpatients generally require 5.5 direct nursing hours per day with an average length of stay of 10–22 days. Rehabilitation hospitals or units must comply with the 3-hour rule, where the patient population is required to tolerate at least 3 hours of therapy per day.

New Coverage Criteria

At the end of July 2009, CMS published the final rules for IRFs for 2010. The final rules adopted a new regulatory framework that clarified the coverage criteria. These new coverage criteria went into effect on January 1, 2010. Figure 6.4 provides these key requirements.

These coverage criteria are intended to ensure that patients who need the intense rehabilitation services that an IRF provides have access to high-quality care. These coverage criteria establish requirements for pre-admission screening of any potential IRF patient, which the facility can then use to document a patient's eligibility for comprehensive rehabilitation services in this type of setting; for post-admission treatment planning requirements; and for ongoing coordination of care requirements.

The specific Medicare coverage requirements include the following:

- Admission criteria that the patient is able and willing to actively participate in an intensive rehabilitation program and is expected to make measurable improvements in functional capacity or adaptation to impairments.
- That IRF services be ordered by a rehabilitation physician with specialized training and experience in rehabilitation services and be coordinated by an interdisciplinary team, including at least a registered nurse with specialized training or experience in rehabilitation, a social worker or case manager (or both), and a licensed or certified therapist from each therapy discipline involved in treating the patient. The rehabilitation physician would be responsible for making the final decisions regarding the patient's treatment in the IRF.

Preadmission Requirements	• IRF shall ensure that each patient's treatment is managed using a coordinated *interdisciplinary* approach to treatment, not just *multidisciplinary*.
	• Expand scope of preadmission assessment to require documentation of the clinical evaluation process that must form the basis of the admission decision.
	• Comprehensive preadmission screening must include an evaluation of the following requirements that a patient must meet to be admitted to an IRF: 　1. patient must be sufficiently stable at time of admission to actively participate in an intensive rehabilitation program; 　2. at the time of admission, the patient must require the active and ongoing therapeutic intervention of at least two therapy disciplines, one of which must be physical therapy or occupational therapy; and 　3. patients generally must require and reasonably be expected to actively participate in at least 3 hours of therapy per day at least 5 days per week and be expected to make measureable improvement that will be of practical value to improve patient's functional capacity or adaptation to impairments. The therapy treatment must begin within 36 hours after patient's admission.
	• An evaluation of each patient's risk for clinical complications is a mandatory part of preadmission screening.
	• Close medical supervision requirement met by having a rehab physician or other licensed treating physician conduct face-to-face visits with the patient a minimum of at least 3 days per week throughout patient's stay.
	• Preadmission screening must be conducted by a qualified clinician designated by a rehab physician within 48 hours immediately preceding the IRF admission.
	• Preadmission screening documentation must be retained in patient's medical record.
	• A rehabilitation physician must review and document his or her concurrence with the findings and results of the preadmission screening.
	• Delete the current post-admission evaluation period.
Post-admission Requirements	• Add requirement for a post-admission evaluation by a rehabilitation physician within 24 hours of admission in order to document the patient's status on admission to the IRF, compare it to that noted in preadmission screening documentation, and begin development of the patient's expected course of treatment that will be completed with input from all of the interdisciplinary team members in the overall plan of care.
	• Require that an individualized overall plan of care be developed for each IRF admission by the end of the fourth day following the patient's admission to the IRF, and retain this plan in the patient's medical record.
Interdisciplinary Team Meeting Requirements	• Increase the required frequency of the interdisciplinary team meeting to at least once per week rather than at least once every two weeks.
	• Broaden the requirements regarding the professional staff that are expected to participate in the interdisciplinary team meetings by mandating professionals from the following disciplines: 　• a rehabilitation physician with specialized training and experience in rehabilitation services; 　• a registered nurse with specialization or experience in rehabilitation; 　• a social worker or case manager (or both); and 　• a licensed or certified therapist from each therapy discipline involved in treating the patient.
	• Require that the rehabilitation physician document concurrence with all decisions made by the interdisciplinary team at each meeting.

FIGURE 6.4

2010 rules—key requirements for inpatient rehabilitation. (*Source:* Murer Consultants based on CMS Rules.)

- A post-admission evaluation to document the status of the patient after admission to the IRF, and comparison of this post-admission screen and the preadmission screening documentation. Using this information, facilities can begin developing an overall plan of care that is designed to meet the individual patient's specific needs. The rule requires the maintenance of the overall plan of care in the patient's medical record. The deadline for completing the overall plan of care is the end of the fourth day following the patient's admission. The final rule does not require the rehabilitation physician to consult with the interdisciplinary team members when developing the post-admission evaluation, although the rule encourages the rehabilitation physician to consider any available input from the interdisciplinary team members.
- That IRFs use qualified personnel to provide required rehabilitation nursing, physical therapy, occupational therapy, plus as-needed speech–language pathology, social services, psychological (including neuropsychological) services, and prosthetic and orthotic services.
- That the interdisciplinary team meet weekly to review the patient's progress and make any needed modifications to the individualized overall plan of care.

Three-Hour Rule

The general threshold for establishing the need for inpatient hospital rehabilitation is that the patient must require and can be reasonably expected to actively participate in and benefit from an intensive rehabilitation therapy program. Under this standard, the intensive therapy program generally consists of at least three hours of therapy (physical therapy, occupational therapy, speech–language pathology, or prosthetics/orthotics therapy) per day, at least five days per week. The three hours per day requirement can be met by a combination of these therapeutic services, although one of the therapeutic services must be physical or occupational therapy.

Criteria for Admission

IRFs have certain criteria for admission including the following:

- Medical necessity must be established for intensive rehabilitation services by a rehabilitation physician with specialized training and experience in rehabilitation.

- Patient must be able and willing to actively participate.
- Close medical supervision by a physician specialized in rehabilitation.
- 24-hour availability of rehabilitative nursing.
- 5.5 direct nursing hours per patient per day.
- A length of stay of 10–22 days.
- A need for an intense level of rehabilitation—3-hour rule.
- Services cannot be performed in a less-intensive setting (e.g., skilled nursing facility or outpatient).
- Multidisciplinary team approach coordinated by a rehabilitation physician with specialized training and experience in rehabilitation services and including at least a registered nurse with specialized training or experience in rehabilitation, a social worker or case manager (or both), and a licensed or certified therapist from each therapy discipline involved. The physician would be responsible for making the final decisions regarding care.
- Patient requires a coordinated program of care.
- 60 percent of patients must fall within one of the specific qualifying conditions (previously, the 75 Percent Rule).
- Documentation by different disciplines must be consistent with respect to a patient's condition.
- Post-admission evaluation and comparison of the post- and pre-screening document.
- A significant practical improvement can be expected.

60 Percent Rule (Previously the 75 Percent Rule)

Inpatient rehabilitation providers are also restricted to treating a specific patient population. As one of the special types of hospitals excluded from the Medicare Inpatient Prospective Payment System, these facilities must admit at least 60 percent of their patients with certain conditions. The purpose of this criterion is to ensure that IRFs are primarily involved in providing intensive rehabilitation services to patients who cannot be served in any other less-intensive rehab setting.

Originally referred to as the 75 Percent Rule, under current regulations the percentage has been frozen at 60 percent. In addition to Medicare patients, these percentages also now apply to Medicare Advantage discharges.

Conditions included within the percentage rules include the following:

1. Stroke
2. Spinal cord injury
3. Congenital deformity
4. Amputation
5. Major multiple trauma
6. Fracture of femur (hip fracture)
7. Brain injury
8. Neurological disorders including multiple sclerosis, motor neuron diseases, polyneuropathy, muscular dystrophy, and Parkinson's disease
9. Burns
10. Active polyarticular rheumatoid arthritis, psoriatic arthritis, and seronegative arthropathies resulting in significant functional impairment of ambulation and other activities of daily living that have not improved after an appropriate, aggressive, and sustained course of outpatient therapy services or services in other less-intensive rehabilitation settings immediately preceding the inpatient rehabilitation admission or that result from a systemic disease activation immediately before admission but have the potential to improve with more intensive rehabilitation.
11. Systemic vasculidities with joint inflammation, resulting in significant functional impairment of ambulation and other activities of daily living that have not improved after an appropriate, aggressive, and sustained course of outpatient therapy services or services in other less-intensive rehabilitation settings immediately preceding the inpatient rehabilitation admission or that results from a systemic disease activation immediately before admission, but have the potential to improve with more intense rehabilitation.
12. Severe or advanced osteoarthritis (osteoarthrosis or degenerative joint disease) involving two or more major weight-bearing joints (elbows, shoulders, hips, or knees), but not counting a joint with a prosthesis with joint deformity and substantial loss of range of motion, atrophy of muscles surrounding the joint, significant functional impairment of ambulation and other activities of daily living that have not improved after the patient has participated in an appropriate, aggressive, and sustained course of outpatient therapy services or services in other less-intensive rehabilitation settings

immediately preceding the inpatient rehabilitation admission but have the potential to improve with more intensive rehab imitation. (A joint replacement by a prosthesis no longer is considered to have osteoarthritis or other arthritis even if this condition was the reason for the joint replacement.)

13. Knee or hip joint replacement or both, during an acute hospitalization immediately preceding the inpatient rehabilitation stay and also meet one or more of the following specific criteria:
    - the patient underwent a bilateral hip or knee replacement during an inpatient hospital stay immediately preceding the IRF admission;
    - the patient is extremely obese, with a body mass index of at least 50 at the time of admission to the IRF; or
    - the patient is age 85 or older at the time of admission to the IRF.

The percentage rule must be met during the rehabilitation facility's cost-reporting period.

Physician Coverage

IRFs must have a medical director that provides services to the unit and to its patients for at least 20 hours per week. The medical director must ensure that there is a preadmission screening process to determine if the patient is likely to benefit significantly from an intensive hospital program. They must also ensure that services are reasonable and necessary, meaning the services cannot be performed in a less-intensive setting such as a skilled nursing facility or an outpatient facility.

Medical Directorship—20 Hours per Week Rule

For the inpatient rehabilitation unit, documenting the hours worked by the unit's medical director can be somewhat thorny because the regulations state that the medical director must provide "services to the unit and to its inpatients for at least 20 hours per week."[*]

The documentation problem often arises when the unit provides services to both inpatients and outpatients. Recognizing that it would be impractical to require the medical director of such a unit to attempt to divide time spent on administrative functions between the inpatient and the outpatient aspects

---

[*] 42 C.F.R. § 412.29(f)(1).

of the unit's program, CMS permits the medical director to count all administrative time toward satisfaction of the 20-hour requirement.* The medical director, however, may allocate to the 20-hour requirement only that portion of time spent furnishing direct patient care that was actually spent treating inpatients.† Thus, it is critically important for the medical director to keep accurate logs of the time spent working for the unit and its patients.

Accurate medical director logs are critical to the hospital from a reimbursement as well as a compliance viewpoint. The regulations provide that physician compensation costs cannot be reimbursed to the hospital unless the physician's time records are maintained "in a form that permits the information to be validated by the intermediary."‡ The CMS *Provider Reimbursement Manual* states, "While we do not require the maintenance of *daily* logs or time records to support provider services rendered by physicians, adequate documentation must be maintained to support the total hours for these services."§

Product Line Specialization

A rehabilitation program is distinguished by its product line orientation. The determination of areas of specialization is directly related to the medical focus of the primary referral hospitals and their medical staffs. A rehabilitation unit within a trauma hospital is more likely to see brain injury and spinal cord patients, whereas a community-based hospital may refer more neurological patients.

A rehabilitation program has the ability to take greater control of its fate and expand its referral base beyond a community radius to a regional presence, through recognition of its competencies in certain areas of rehabilitation medicine.

Inpatient Rehabilitation—Payment Structure

Rehabilitation patients are paid based on a case mix group (CMG). The CMG is a patient classification system that groups together inpatient medical rehabilitation patients who are expected to have similar resource utilization needs and outcomes.

---

* CMS Provider Reimbursement Manual, Part 1, § 3001.7D.
† Ibid.
‡ 42 C.F.R. § 415.60(g)(1).
§ CMS Provider Reimbursement Manual § 2182.3E4.

TABLE 6.3

Inpatient Rehabilitation Payment Examples for
Stroke Patients

Stroke Case Mix	Weight	Payment
CMG 101 High Tier	.8035	$11,136
CMG 101 Medium Tier	.7197	$9,975
CMG 101 Low Tier	.6454	$8,945
CMG 101 No Comorbidities	.6096	$8,449

Source: CMS 2011 base rate of $13,860.

The patient assessment instrument (PAI) is used to classify a patient into a CMG. Each CMG has different comorbidity tiers and weights that are multiplied by the rehab hospital or unit's base rate to arrive at the payment.

For example, stroke has a total of 40 different CMG categories from 101 to 110, each with four levels and weights. These weights are applied to the 2011 Budget Neutral rate of $13,860 to arrive at payment (see Table 6.3).

Rehabilitation inpatients can also qualify for high cost outlier payments after exceeding a pre-determined threshold. For 2011, this threshold amount for those complex cases is $11,410.

SKILLED NURSING FACILITY/UNIT

Overview

SNUs and skilled nursing facilities (SNFs) are designed to treat patients needing 4.5 direct nursing hours per day. When health systems do not have alternative venues of care, SNUs may be forced to take higher acuity patients, resulting in higher direct nursing hours per patient day. Unfortunately, an SNU is not reimbursed to reflect these higher nursing costs.

It is important that the health system adopt and carefully follow specific admission criteria to ensure that those patients admitted to a skilled nursing unit can easily be managed with the available resources.

Admission Criteria

SNUs have certain criteria for admission:

- Medicare patients' preadmission requirements for an SNU are that the patients must have been hospitalized for medically necessary inpatient hospital care for at least three consecutive calendar days prior to coming to the skilled unit.

- A patient must require skilled nursing or skilled rehabilitation services or both on a daily basis.
- The services must be ordered by a physician.
- The services must require the skills of technical professional personnel such as nurses, physical therapists, occupational therapists, and speech pathologists or audiologists.
- There is *no* 3-hour rule relating to hours of therapy per day.
- The services are furnished directly by or under the supervision of the personnel listed above.
- The services must be furnished for a condition for which the patient received inpatient hospital services.
- The daily skilled services must be ones that, as a practical matter, can only be provided in an SNU on an inpatient basis.

Skilled Nursing Physician Care

The attending physician must be involved in the development of the patient's comprehensive care plan and must be notified of lab, radiology, and other diagnostic findings relevant to the patient in addition to any drug irregularities the patient suffers. Regulations specify that the SNU must designate a physician to serve as its medical director who is responsible for the implementation of patient care policies and the coordination of medical care at the unit or facility.

Skilled Nursing Payment Structure

SNFs are covered by Medicare Part A if the skilled nursing facility stay follows within 30 days of a hospitalization of 3 days or more and is medically necessary. Skilled nursing Medicare days are limited to 100 days per benefit period with a copayment required for days 21 to 100. A benefit period begins when the patient first enters the hospital and ends when there is a break of at least 60 consecutive days since an inpatient hospital stay or skilled nursing was provided.

SNUs are paid based on an assigned resource utilization group (RUG) category which is updated annually with labor and nonlabor portions. These amounts are applied to the unit's individual wage index factor.

TABLE 6.4

Payment Examples Based on RUG Category

Example RUG Categories	Payment
RUC—Ultra High Rehab	$634.27
CC2—Pneumonia, Dehydration	$299.79

Source: CMS 2011 Urban RUG rates.

Each of the RUG categories falls into several major types, including rehabilitation, extensive services, clinically complex, and others. The amount of rehabilitation and/or services provided will determine which RUG category the patient is assigned. For example:

Rehab, Ultra High
- Structure 2 disciplines
- 2.5 hours, 5 days per week
- Typical diagnosis: stroke/neuro

Each RUG category has a different payment assigned to it, as is demonstrated in Table 6.4.

The Difference between Comprehensive Inpatient Rehabilitation and Skilled Nursing

In many instances case managers, payers, and even patients seem to believe there is little difference between comprehensive inpatient rehabilitation and subacute (skilled) rehabilitation. Payers will insist the patient be treated at a subacute unit primarily on the basis of the payment structure. This is truly a disservice to the patients, since they are not receiving the appropriate level of care at a critical point in their recovery process.

Picture a 20-year-old pulmonary patient on a ventilator. This young man is denied acute rehabilitation for reconditioning because a subacute bed was available. A 50-year-old stroke patient is told she does not meet criteria for comprehensive inpatient rehabilitation but she is eligible for subacute care. In both examples, payment was the deciding factor. Payment for subacute rehabilitation is less than comprehensive inpatient rehabilitation. Skilled rehab is paid under a RUGs category payment and based on a lesser level of care including nursing and therapy.

These two venues should not be considered interchangeable. A patient who is truly appropriate for a comprehensive inpatient rehabilitation

TABLE 6.5

Comparisons: Comprehensive Rehab versus Skilled Nursing

Comprehensive Inpatient Rehabilitation	Skilled Nursing
• Specific diagnosis to meet 60% rule • Paid under a rehab CMG based on primary condition with tier level based on certain comorbidities • Can be CARF accredited • Minimum 3 hours therapy per day • Provided at least 5–6 days per week • Physicians' services 6 days per week with 24/7 internal medicine coverage availability • Patient appropriate for comprehensive inpatient rehabilitation is not appropriate for a skilled rehab level of care	• Less intense rehab • Paid under a RUG category • Medium rehab RUG = 0.5 hours therapy per day • Ultra-high rehab RUG = 2.5 hours per day • Patient appropriate for a subacute/skilled rehab level is not appropriate for comprehensive inpatient rehabilitation

Source: Murer Consultants.

setting, in that he or she requires 24 hours of nursing with 3 hours of therapy per day at least 5–6 days per week, would not be appropriate for a subacute (skilled nursing) rehabilitation level of care (Table 6.5).

Subacute rehabilitation patients need an inpatient setting but at a far lower intensity than comprehensive inpatient rehabilitation. In fact, some patients may transfer to a skilled/subacute facility for treatment once their stay at the inpatient rehabilitation facility is complete.

OUTPATIENT REHABILITATION AND HOME HEALTH

Outpatient Rehabilitation

If a patient is appropriate for neither comprehensive inpatient rehabilitation nor skilled nursing, but could benefit from additional rehabilitation services, then outpatient rehabilitation or home health may be an option.

Outpatient rehabilitation provides physical therapy, occupational therapy, and/or speech therapy to patients who can travel to receive their therapy. Outpatient services can meet the needs of patients who have moderate to severe limitations.

Therapists must establish separate and distinct discipline-specific goals for patients who receive services in more than one discipline (e.g., physical therapy and occupational therapy), and treatment may not be duplicated. Therapists must take care that the use of modalities is not excessive and to ensure that all treatments are appropriately documented.

Home Health

Home health provides skilled care in the patient's home and can include nursing, physical therapy, occupational therapy, and speech/language therapy. Patients are required to be "homebound" as a condition of eligibility for these services. Generally, patients receiving this care are recovering after their stay at a hospital or nursing home.

Medicare pays home health agencies through a prospective payment system that provides for higher payment rates based on the patient's needs. These rates are based on relevant clinical data taken from the required patient assessment.

This amount is adjusted for the health condition and care needs of the beneficiary. The payment is also adjusted based on the wage index. Home Health PPS will provide the home health agency with payment for each 60-day episode of care.

Hospice

Hospice provides care to terminally ill patients. Generally, hospice care begins when a person's life expectancy is six months or less. Hospice can be provided at inpatient facilities or within the patient's home. Hospice is a venue of care in which the physical, spiritual, social, and economic needs of the terminally ill patient and his or her family are addressed.

There are a number of physicians who adamantly refuse to consider hospice. They believe hospice represents a failure on their part, and they refuse to use this venue of care.

This is unfortunate for two reasons. First, the end-of-life patient remains in an acute level of care for which payment to the facility is no longer covered. If the patient is moved to a hospice level of care, either inpatient or at home, a separate payment system is available for the care.

Second, hospice has a proper role to play in the care of end-of-life patients. Hospice provides compassionate care and addresses the spiritual needs of the patients and their families. Hospice regards dying as a part of living and is responsive to the individual needs of the family. These are two very important aspects that are not typically addressed in any other venue of care.

The concept behind post acute venues of care is placing the patient in the appropriate venue based on medical need and expected length of stay for the proper reimbursement.

Case management plays an important function in ensuring placement of the right patient in the right post acute venue in the timeliest manner possible. Not only is this better for the patient, but it is also better for the financial bottom line of the health system. By moving patients to the appropriate post acute venue, the system receives additional revenue rather than allowing patients to sit in the acute venue for no additional reimbursement.

Case management should be at the epicenter of an integrated health system. Chapter 7 focuses on how case management can appropriately move patients from venue to venue once their short-term acute stay is complete. The chapter also includes several case studies with the movement of patients through the continuum of care.

CHAPTER 6 ACTION ITEMS

- Discuss the post acute venues in your health system.
- Each case manager should have a better understanding of each post acute venue based on the information provided in this chapter.
- Is hospice used appropriately at your facility?

7

Case Management at the Epicenter of an Integrated Health System

---

THE EPICENTER OF AN INTEGRATED HEALTH SYSTEM

Case management is at the epicenter of an integrated healthcare system (Figure 7.1). Case management moves the patient at the right time and to the right place to support medical necessity and receive appropriate payment.

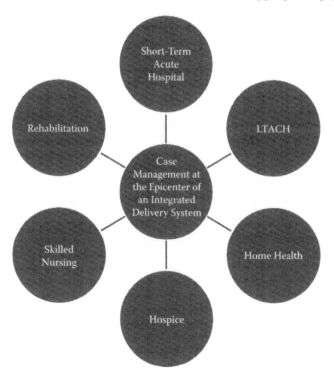

FIGURE 7.1
Epicenter of integrated healthcare.

MODELS

There are several models of case management used by hospitals and health systems across the country. Some of these models include the following:

- Unit Based
- Physician Based
- Service Line
- Payer Based
- Disease Management
- Gate Keeping

There are also specifically developed models often referred to as *hybrid models* of case management.

THE HYBRID MODEL OF CASE MANAGEMENT

In the hybrid model of case management, the case managers are cross-trained and understand the multiple venues of care. All case managers have a general knowledge of all the venues of care within the system in which they operate.

It is important for all case managers to have a clinical background. It is generally recommended that the case management team be made up of a 75/25 mix where 75 percent have a nursing/clinical background and the remaining 25 percent come with social worker expertise.

Each case manager should be articulate in the regulatory and financial implications related to each venue. All case managers should be trained in the appropriateness of each venue of post acute care including the admission criteria and discharge triggers for each venue.

In this hybrid model (see Figure 7.2), each case manager is assigned to one of three areas:

- Primary Referral Experts—One-third of the case managers are assigned to one of the primary post acute venues, for example, inpatient rehabilitation, skilled nursing, long-term acute care hospital, or home health. These individuals are case finders for these post acute

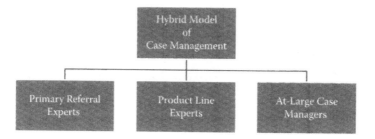

FIGURE 7.2
Hybrid model of case management. (*Source:* Murer Consultants, Inc.)

venues and work closely with other case managers to identify and move patients in a timely manner.

- Product Line Experts—One-third of the case managers are trained in specific product lines, for example, orthopedic, cardiac, or critical care product lines.
- At-Large Case Managers—One-third of the case managers are generalists who are familiar with all options within the continuum but generally see patients who are being admitted to hospital units or who, after their acute care stay, are returning home or to skilled care. These case managers are generally assigned to the emergency room or to medical/surgical units.

SEAMLESS PROTOCOLS

It is important for a health system to develop seamless protocols from acute inpatient to post acute venues of care. These protocols determine when it's time to move the patient to the next level of care. It is important to know when a stroke patient should move from the ICU at the hospital to the medical/surgical floor to inpatient rehabilitation, skilled nursing, or home.

For example, at the short-term acute hospital, protocols should be in place whereby whenever a stroke patient presents to the acute care hospital, the inpatient rehabilitation hospital/unit is automatically contacted to evaluate the patient as a possible referral. Discharge triggers are also in place at the inpatient rehabilitation hospital/unit to instruct the unit to discharge the patient who no longer requires 24-hour nursing and thereby, according to regulation, needs to move to a lesser level of care.

In order to distinguish among and between venue options, the case manager must become an expert in the intended distinctions of each venue and be versatile as to each venue's capabilities and outcome expectations.

DISCHARGE TRIGGERS

The most judicious method of applying a multicontinuum strategy is by using triggers from the most restrictive environment as the admission criteria of the lesser restrictive venue. A case study model has been used to depict the discharge trigger methodology whereby the patient is admitted to the next level of care of the continuum when the outcome expectations for acute care have been met. The two most essential discharge measures for acute care are

- when the patient's condition is no longer erratic and/or
- when surgery is not imminent.

For example, as it relates to a rehabilitation-directed diagnosis, such as stroke, when the two previously identified discharge triggers of acute care are met, the patient may then be referred to the less restrictive, less costly environment of subacute care when the primary objective is the medical management of the patient, until such point when the rehabilitation potential is optimal and the patient can best benefit from a physical/functional restorative care program.

Subsequently, in keeping with this method, the discharge trigger from the comprehensive inpatient rehabilitation unit to the Medical Day Hospital™ should be when the patient is no longer in need of 24-hour rehabilitation nursing services and daily physician intervention. When such a condition exists, the patient should be discharged to an intensive day program where areas of cognitive training, community reentry, and advanced physical functioning and psychosocial issues can be addressed.

Case management is the vehicle of patient flow and optimal utilization of available resources. Under an integrated health system, patients should move seamlessly from one venue of care to the next based on their medical needs. Figures 7.6 and 7.7 at the end of this chapter are examples of how a patient could ideally be moved from venue to venue.

CASE STUDIES

Case Study One (Figure 7.3) shows how a patient with an Intracranial Hemorrhage or Cerebral Infarction w/MCC, diagnosis-related group (DRG) 64, moves from an acute hospital stay to a skilled nursing unit to a Medical Day Hospital™. The patient initially stays 6 days in the acute hospital. In Case Study One the patient is a frail 76-year-old who cannot tolerate an intensive rehab program. At discharge from the short-term acute care hospital, the patient moves to a skilled nursing unit for 16 days to regain strength. Once his condition improves, the patient discharges home but continues therapy three times per week at a Medical Day Hospital™ for 8 weeks of intensive outpatient therapy.

In Case Study Two (Figure 7.4), the patient is a younger stroke victim who is 66 years old and appropriate for a comprehensive inpatient rehabilitation unit. The patient stays in the acute hospital 6 days and is then discharged to the inpatient rehab unit for intensive inpatient therapy. This is followed by a 6-week outpatient program in a Medical Day Hospital™ setting, and then a 3-month fitness/wellness program.

In Case Study Three (Figure 7.5), a 28-year-old major multiple trauma patient is admitted to the hospital via the emergency department. The patient is initially treated in the hospital ICU for 2 days, followed by a 4-day stay in the medical/surgical unit. In this example, the patient requires an intensive extended stay and is discharged to a long-term acute care hospital where the patient receives *aftercare* for musculoskeletal and tissue injuries for an additional 23 days. At discharge the patient needs less intensive treatment and is sent to a skilled nursing facility for 2 weeks prior to discharging home.

These three case studies demonstrate the appropriate use of the continuum of care.

APPROPRIATE MOVEMENT OF THE PATIENT

Figures 7.6 and 7.7 demonstrate the financial implications of a patient who does not (Figure 7.6) and a patient who does (Figure 7.7) move appropriately through the continuum. In Figure 7.6, the patient remains

Case Study One

Continuum of Care – Case Study
Functional Outcome per Venue

STROKE – DRG 64
Intracranial Hemorrhage or
Cerebral Infarction w/MCC

Copyrighted by Murer Consultants, Inc.
Joliet, Illinois

PROFILE:
• 76-year-old accountant

DIAGNOSIS
• CVA
• Left Hemi

DEFICITS:
• Moderate swallowing
• Moderate spasticity & flaccidity
• Mild perceptual deficit
• Moderate impaired mobility
• Mild cognitive impairment
• Incontinent bowel/bladder
• Moderate language impairment
• Hypertension
• Atrial fibrillation

ACUTE CARE HOSPITAL
LOS 6 DAYS

DRG 64– GM LOS 5.1
• Medical condition no longer erratic
• No surgery pending
• Major diagnostics completed
• No trach or vent

SKILLED NURSING UNIT
LOS 16 Days

Discharge Goal:
Able to tolerate & benefit from restorative care provided in an ambulatory setting

Functional Outcome:
• Maintenance of medical stability
• Family orientation to safety & effects of the disability
• Basic DME identified & process for procurement initiated
• Patient & family oriented to the discharge destination
• Nutritional status stable with awareness of recommended diet
• Strong family/caregiver system in place
• Able to transfer from bed to chair
• Moderate assistance with basic toileting and hygiene
• Able to follow commands
• Medical management of co-morbidities

MEDICAL DAY HOSPITAL
LOS 8 Weeks
3x Per Week

Discharge Goal:
Able to function safely at home and in the community.

Functional Outcome:
• Restored functional mobility
• Minimal assistance with ADLs
• Able to communicate basic needs
• Stable modified diet
• Patient routinely exercises coping skills
• Home adaptations identified and in process
• Splinting and orthotics competed
• Patient & family demonstrate ability to manage environmental barriers
• Patient able to participate in at least one community outing per week
• Patient driving skills assessed as appropriate
• Able to manage health risk factors independently or with caregiver
• Family aware of residual effects of disability with recognition of available coping mechanisms

FIGURE 7.3
Case Study One. (*Source:* Murer Consultants, Inc.)

Case Study Two

Continuum of Care – Case Study
Functional Outcome Per Venue

STROKE – DRG 64
Intracranial Hemorrhage or
Cerebral Infarction w/MCC

Copyrighted by Murer Consultants, Inc.
Joliet, Illinois

PROFILE:
• 66-year-old accountant

DIAGNOSIS
• CVA
• Left Hemi

DEFICITS:
• Low grade fever
• Aspiration pneumonia
• Moderate swallowing
• Moderate spasticity & flaccidity
• Mild perceptual deficit
• Severe impaired mobility
• Moderate cognitive impairment
• Incontinent bowel/bladder
• Severe sensory motor dysfunction
• Short-term memory loss
• Moderate language impairment
• Moderate comprehension of impairment
• Mild maladaptive behavior

ACUTE CARE HOSPITAL
LOS 6 DAYS

DRG 64–GMLOS 5.1
• Medical condition no longer erratic
• No surgery pending
• No trach or other mechanical respiratory devices
• Family oriented to restorative care process within multiple venues
• Able to tolerate minimum three hours of therapy
• Identified rehab potential

COMPREHENSIVE INPATIENT UNIT
LOS 22 Days

Discharge Goal:
Return to home with intensive day program.

Functional Outcome:
• Ambulates with moderate assistance with adaptive aids
• Continent of both bowel and bladder
• Skin integrity maintained
• Basic communication skills for primary needs
• Swallowing difficulty resolved
• Control of health risk factors
• No major respiratory involvement
• Maintenance of medical stability
• No longer requires IV antibiotics
• Normal nutritional status
• Family orientation
• Strong family support and communication

MEDICAL DAY HOSPITAL™
LOS 6 Weeks

Discharge Goal:
Community and leisure time reintegration.

Functional Outcome:
• Ambulates independently with adaptive aids
• Independent use of wheelchair to avoid fatigue
• Performs ADL activities with little to no assistance including dressing, grooming, bathing, hygiene, and toileting
• Occasional memory lapse but consistently responds to cues
• Intermediate communication skills, expressive and reception to simple sentences
• Enhanced coping skills
• Reduction of pain caused by spasticity
• Manages occasional pain through identified techniques
• Good safety techniques
• Endures up to 8 hours of daily activity
• Family demonstrates knowledge & support of patient's residual deficits

FITNESS/WELLNESS PROGRAM
LOS 3 Months

Discharge Goal:
Develop healthy lifestyle habits & minimize risk factors.

Functional Outcome:
• Able to continue healthy lifestyle without supervision
• Able to transfer customized fitness program to community health club
• Managed risk factors
• No longer smokes
• Cholesterol under 200
• Blood pressure normal
• Weight within 10–15 pounds of desired range

FIGURE 7.4
Case Study Two. (*Source:* Murer Consultants, Inc.)

Case Study Three

Continuum of Care – Case Study
Functional Outcome per Venue

MAJOR MULTIPLE TRAUMA – DRG 963

Other Multiple Significant Trauma
w/MCC

Copyrighted by Murer Consultants, Inc.
Joliet, Illinois

HOSPITAL EMERGENCY ROOM → **HOSPITAL ICU** 2 Day LOS → **ACUTE HOSPITAL** 4 Day LOS → **LONG TERM ACUTE CARE HOSPITAL** 23 Day LOS → **SKILLED NURSING FACILITY** 15 Day LOS

PROFILE:
• 28-year-old middle manager
• Employed at large company
• Commercially insured
• Motor vehicle accident

DIAGNOSIS
• Major multiple trauma with broken ribs, punctured lung, and respiratory distress
• Neurological complications
• Orthopedic complications

DEFICITS:
• Dislocated right shoulder
• Fractures in both lower extremities
• Fractures of right forearm
• Ataxic dysarthria
• Bladder dysfunction
• Short-term memory loss
• Emotional trauma due to accident
• Acute pain from injuries

DRG 963–GMLOS 6.0
• Patient no longer considered in critical condition
• Respiration stable without assistive devices
• Fully conscious
• Medically stable
• No impending surgeries
• Casts in place on affected limbs

DRG 559–Aftercare, Musculoskeletal System & Connective Tissue w/ MCC, GMLOS 25.6 (21.3)

Discharge Goal:
Return to home or custodial residential level of care

Functional Outcome:
• No respiratory involvement
• No major medical complications
• Infection free
• Continence of bowel
• Continence of bladder with catheter
• Reduction of pain caused by spasticity
• Normal nutritional status
• Skin integrity maintained
• Mobility with maximum assistance with adaptive aids
• Performs basic ADL skills with assistance in the area of toileting & hygiene
• Maximum assistance for ADL skills of dressing & grooming
• Maximum assistance with bathing
• Basic communication skills for primary needs
• Basic coping skills
• Good receptive language
• Orthotics for motor control
• Family oriented to residual effects of disability
• Strong family support & communication

Discharge Goal:
Return to home

Functional Outcome:
• Remains free of serious infection
• Ambulates with assistive devices
• Independent in basic ADL of toileting, feeding, hygiene, & dressing using non-complex garments
• ADL with assistance in bathing, dressing with complex garments, & grooming
• Coping skills to manage pain
• Motivated on outpatient basis if appropriate

FIGURE 7.5

Case Study Three. (*Source:* Murer Consultants, Inc.)

in the short-term acute care hospital for 20 days, which is 9 days over the Medicare DRG projected arithmetic mean length of stay (AMLOS). This causes the hospital to accumulate $22,500 in uncompensated care. The patient discharges to a long-term acute care hospital. However, the extended 20-day stay at the short-term hospital caused a short stay outlier at the long-term acute care hospital.

In this example both venues suffer financially when the patient is not moved appropriately. The short-term acute care hospital has uncompensated care, and long-term acute care hospital incurs a short stay outlier payment since the patient did not stay longer than the 5/6 long-term care DRG (LTC-DRG).

In Figure 7.7, the patient stays in the short-term acute care hospital for 5 days and then discharges to the long-term acute care hospital for 21 days. The patient stays appropriately at both venues.

The short stay hospital does not accumulate any uncompensated care. The patient stays more than the 5/6 length of stay at the long-term acute care hospital and receives the full payment at this venue as well. It's a win–win situation for both venues.

It is important to anticipate the patient's length of stay at each venue of care. Doing so allows one to monitor where patients are in their stay and allows discharge planning to begin at admission.

The next chapter looks at the DRG system. It takes a close look at reimbursement based on levels of severity. It also discusses the importance of ensuring that the patient's condition and comorbidities are documented appropriately in the patient's chart.

Chapter 8 also discusses assigning a working DRG, which allows everyone responsible for the care of the patient to know where the patient is in the anticipated length of stay.

THE SHORT-TERM ACUTE CARE HOSPITAL

DRG 237
Major Cardiovascular Procedures w/MCC or
Thoracic Aortic Aneurysm Repair
Short-Term Acute Payment: $26,803
AMLOS*: 10.1 days

THE LONG-TERM ACUTE CARE HOSPITAL (LTACH)

DRG 682
Renal Failure w/MCC
LTC-PPS Payment: $36,004
GMLOS: 23.1/19.3 (5/6)

Facts:
- Patient stayed at short-term acute care hospital for a total of 20 days, or 9 days over AMLOS
- Days over caused short-term hospital to accumulate $22,542 in uncompensated care loss
- Patient was appropriate for a LTACH since eventually admitted to LTACH with DRG 682 for 13 days
- Patient would have had a short-term outlier applied since stay at LTACH was less than the 5/6 GMLOS

Missed Opportunity
- Had patient been moved appropriately, short-term hospital would not have had an uncompensated care loss of $22,542.
- LTACH could have had a length of stay of 22 days instead of 13, which would have meant a full DRG payment of $36,004 rather than a short-term outlier payment of $24,002.

	Payment	Potential Payment
Short-Term Acute	$26,803	$26,803
Uncompensated Care Loss for Acute Stay	-($22,542)	
LTACH Payment	$24,002	$36,004
TOTAL	$28,263	$62,807
MISSED OPPORTUNITY = $34,544		

*Not a transfer DRG.
** Payments based on 2011 National Base Rates

FIGURE 7.6

Financial implication of a patient who does not move appropriately. (*Source:* Murer Consultants, Inc.)

THE SHORT-TERM ACUTE HOSPITAL

DRG 391
Esophagitis, Gastroenteritis & Misc. Digestive Disorders w/MCC
Short Term Acute Payment: $5,946
AMLOS*: 5.1 days

THE LONG-TERM ACUTE CARE HOSPITAL (LTACH)

DRG 640
Nutritional & Misc. Metabolic Disorders w/MCC
LTC-PPS Payment: $34,570
GMLOS: 23.1/19.3 (5/6)

Facts:
• Patient stayed at short-term acute hospital for 5 days
• No days over, therefore no uncompensated care
• Patient stayed 21 days at LTACH qualifying for full LTC-PPS payment

	Payment	Potential Payment
Short-Term Acute	$5,964	$5,964
Uncompensated Care Loss for Acute Stay	$0	$0
LTACH Payment	$34,570	$34,570
TOTAL	$40,573	$40,573

*Not a transfer DRG.
** Payments based on 2011 National Base Rates.

FIGURE 7.7

Financial implication of a patient who does move appropriately. (*Source:* Murer Consultants, Inc.)

CHAPTER 7 ACTION ITEMS

- Develop a case study from your experience modeled after the examples provided in this chapter.
- Provide an example of a patient who moved inappropriately through the system and a second example of the financial benefit when a patient is moved appropriately.

8

Diagnosis-Related Group Review

OVERVIEW

The inpatient prospective payment system is the payment structure for short-term acute care hospitals. Based on the information provided in the patient's medical record, each patient is assigned to a major diagnostic category (MDC), which is further broken down by a diagnosis-related group (DRG) (Table 8.1).

MAJOR DIAGNOSTIC CATEGORY

First, each patient is assigned to an MDC category. All patients are assigned to one of 25 MDCs based on their principal diagnoses. Most MDCs are organized by major body system and/or are associated with a particular medical specialty. All DRGs fall under one of these MDC categories. MDCs are broken into two sections—surgical or medical:

- The surgical section includes all surgical conditions based upon an operating room procedure.
- The medical section includes all diagnostic conditions based upon diagnosis codes.

In addition to the 25 MDC categories, there is a Pre-MDC category and a category associated with All MDCs. The Pre-MDCs include DRGs that consist of cases grouped by surgical procedure instead of principal diagnosis. For example, DRG 1, Heart Transplant or Implant of Heart

TABLE 8.1

Major Diagnostic Categories (MDCs)

MDC #	Description
MDC 1	Diseases and Disorders of the Nervous System
MDC 2	Diseases and Disorders of the Eye
MDC 3	Diseases and Disorders of the Ear, Nose, Mouth, and Throat
MDC 4	Diseases and Disorders of the Respiratory System
MDC 5	Diseases and Disorders of the Circulatory System
MDC 6	Diseases and Disorders of the Digestive System
MDC 7	Diseases and Disorders of the Hepatobiliary System and Pancreas
MDC 8	Diseases and Disorders of the Musculoskeletal System and Connective Tissue
MDC 9	Diseases and Disorders of the Skin, Subcutaneous Tissue, and Breast
MDC 10	Endocrine, Nutritional, and Metabolic Diseases and Disorders
MDC 11	Diseases and Disorders of the Kidney and Urinary Tract
MDC 12	Diseases and Disorders of the Male Reproductive System
MDC 13	Diseases and Disorders of the Female Reproductive System
MDC 14	Pregnancy, Childbirth, and the Puerperium
MDC 15	Newborns and Other Neonates with Conditions Originating in the Perinatal Period
MDC 16	Diseases and Disorders of Blood and Blood-Forming Organs and Immunological Disorders
MDC 17	Myeloproliferative Diseases and Disorders and Poorly Differentiated Neoplasms
MDC 18	Infectious and Parasitic Diseases
MDC 19	Mental Diseases and Disorders
MDC 20	Alcohol/Drug Use and Alcohol/Drug-Induced Organic Mental Disorders
MDC 21	Injury, Poisoning, and Toxic Effects of Drugs
MDC 22	Burns
MDC 23	Factors Influencing Health Status and Other Contacts with Health Services
MDC 24	Multiple Significant Trauma
MDC 25	Human Immunodeficiency Virus Infections
Pre-MDC	
All MDC	

Source: CMS.

Assist System with MCC (major complication/comorbidity); DRG 6, Liver Transplant without MCC; and DRG 4, Tracheostomy with Mechanical Ventilation 96+ hours or Principal Diagnosis Except Face, Mouth, and Neck without Major OR are included in this Pre-MDC category.

Under DRGs associated with All MDCs are cases that have operating room procedures unrelated to the principal diagnosis or those assigned an invalid principal diagnosis.

DIAGNOSIS-RELATED GROUPS

The patient's condition is further identified by a DRG. DRGs are assigned based on the following:

- Principal and secondary diagnosis or procedure codes
- Patient's sex
- Patient's discharge status
- Presence or absence of major complications and comorbidities (MCCs) and/or presence or absence of complications and comorbidities (CC)
- In neonates, the birth weight

The DRG system is to classify hospital cases into one group that is expected to use similar hospital resources. This system was developed for Medicare as part of the prospective payment system. However, a number of managed care and commercial providers, and some Medicaid providers, mirror this system.

DRGs have been used since 1983 to determine how much Medicare pays the hospital, since patients within each category are similar clinically and are expected to use the same level of hospital resources.

Beginning in October 2007, Medicare adopted a new DRG system for short-term and long-term acute care hospitals to better recognize comorbidities affecting a patient's illness. The Medicare severity diagnosis-related groups (MS-DRGs) take into account all aspects of the patient's condition and/or illness by providing higher payments for sicker patients.

There are currently 746 DRGs into which a patient condition can be grouped. DRGs range from 1 to 999. Each October 1, Medicare adjusts the DRG relative weight, arithmetic mean length of stay (AMLOS), and geometric mean length of stay (GMLOS). In addition, new International Classification of Diseases, 9th Revision, Clinical Modification (ICD-9-CM) codes are added into the existing DRGs, and in some years new DRGs are added or the narrative description of existing DRGs may change.

The introduction of these complications and comorbidities provided health systems a new opportunity for appropriate reimbursement. This new system relies heavily on precise physician documentation for accurate coding. The attention to detail has a significant impact on each individual case. The payment can vary by thousands of dollars based on whether a patient has no CC or MCC, has CC, or has MCC.

With the introduction of complications and comorbidities, there is an opportunity for appropriate reimbursement subject to precise physician documentation and accurate coding.

With or without MCC and CC

The DRGs are further subdivided into three groups, which will be the basis of payment:

- MS-DRG with MCC—*highest* level of severity.
- MS-DRG with CC—presence of a CC assigns the discharge to a higher weighted DRG.
- MS-DRG without CC—diagnosis codes do not significantly affect severity of illness and resource use.

For example, renal failure has three severity levels:

- DRG 682: Renal failure with MCC.
- DRG 683: Renal failure with CC.
- DRG 684: Renal failure without CC/MCC

The Centers for Medicare and Medicaid Services (CMS) has developed a detailed list of these MCC and CC conditions for assignment of hospital cases to appropriate DRGs. When a CC or MCC is present as a secondary diagnosis, it may affect DRG assignment.

The DRG system bases reimbursement on levels of severity; thus, if a patient has a severe condition or comorbidity, the physician *must* document this in the chart. Physician documentation must be

- Accurate
- Descriptive
- Complete

The documentation must not overstate or understate the medical assessment. It must not incorrectly identify complicating conditions. If it is not documented, it did not happen. As evidenced by Figures 8.1–8.5, it is imperative for physicians to ensure accurate and detailed documentation in patient charts.

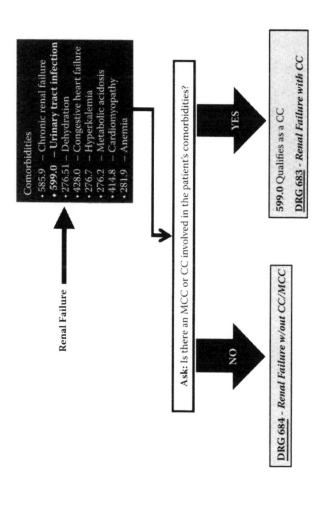

FIGURE 8.1

Example: Effects comorbidities have on the DRG assignment. (*Source:* Murer Consultants, Inc.)

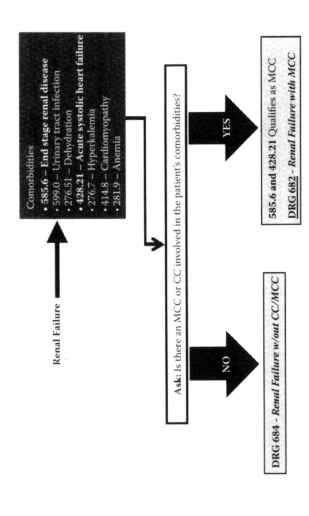

FIGURE 8.2

Example: Effects comorbidities have on the DRG assignment. (*Source:* Murer Consultants, Inc.)

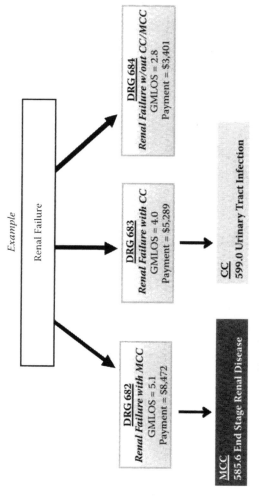

Example

Renal Failure

DRG 682
Renal Failure with MCC
GMLOS = 5.1
Payment = $8,472

DRG 683
Renal Failure with CC
GMLOS = 4.0
Payment = $5,289

DRG 684
Renal Failure w/out CC/MCC
GMLOS = 2.8
Payment = $3,401

<u>MCC</u>
585.6 End Stage Renal Disease

<u>CC</u>
599.0 Urinary Tract Infection

Note: Payment is based on the 2011 National Base Rate

FIGURE 8.3
Comparison DRGs 682–683–684. (*Source:* Murer Consultants, Inc.)

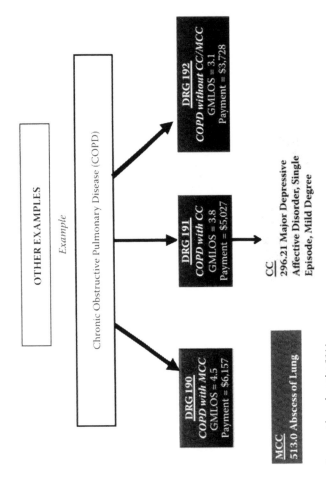

OTHER EXAMPLES

Example

Chronic Obstructive Pulmonary Disease (COPD)

DRG 190
COPD with MCC
GMLOS = 4.5
Payment = $6,157

DRG 191
COPD with CC
GMLOS = 3.8
Payment = $5,027

DRG 192
COPD without CC/MCC
GMLOS = 3.1
Payment = $3,728

MCC
513.0 Abscess of Lung

CC
296.21 Major Depressive
Affective Disorder, Single
Episode, Mild Degree

Payment based on the 2011
National Base Rate

FIGURE 8.4
Comparison DRGs 190–191–192. (*Source:* Murer Consultants, Inc.)

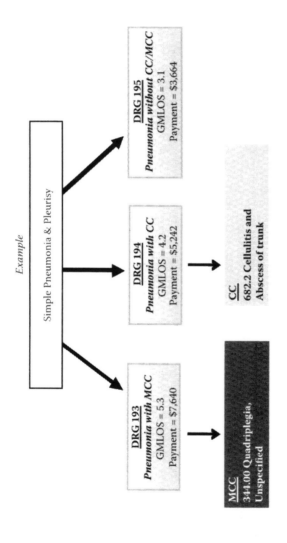

FIGURE 8.5

Comparison DRGs 193–194–195. (*Source:* Murer Consultants, Inc.)

For example, renal failure has several DRGs that could be assigned. The most appropriate DRG depends on the patient's comorbidities or lack thereof. Once renal failure is determined, the next step is to determine the relevant comorbidities. Is there an MCC or a CC involved? If the answer is no, then DRG 684, Renal Failure without CC/MCC, may be appropriate. If there are CCs involved, then DRG 683, Renal Failure with CC, may apply. If the patient's comorbidities qualify as an MCC, then DRG 682, Renal Failure with MCC, applies (see Figures 8.1, 8.2, and 8.3). Other MS-DRGs have similar subcategories. Please refer to the examples in Figures 8.4 and 8.5.

PROJECTING THE DRG

Each year CMS looks at thousands of cases assigned to specific DRGs and determines the anticipated length of stay based on actual care provided. It seems reasonable that assigning a *working DRG* based on these projections from Medicare makes sense.

Assigning a working DRG to a patient has many benefits. It allows everyone involved in the patient's care to have an understanding of the patient's anticipated length of stay. Anticipating the patient's length of stay can be instrumental in developing an appropriate plan of care. This allows the caregiver to know when the patient is approaching movement to the next venue of care (Figure 8.6).

The Sticky Note

Most compliance officers are comfortable with the case management team using the *working DRG sticky note*. The working DRG number, its description, the projected length of stay, and the patient's admit date and anticipated discharge date should be placed prominently on the patient's chart. This allows everyone involved in the patient's care easy access to where the

> 1. Anticipate the patient's length of stay.
> 2. Assist in developing a plan of care
> 3. Recognize when it's time to move to the next level of care.

FIGURE 8.6
Projecting the working DRG.

patient is in his or her discharge of care. It also lets everyone know where patients are in relation to where they *should be* at this point in their stay.

ASSIGNING A DIFFERENT DRG

The short-term acute care hospital and the long-term acute care hospital both utilize the DRG payment system. The DRG system contains many DRGs that are nearly identical in terms of the diagnoses and/or procedures they included. Generally, if a patient requires an extended stay beyond the AMLOS in the short-term acute hospital, the patient has had some type of episode, reaction, or illness that caused the need for additional medical care.

For example, a patient is admitted to the hospital with pneumonia and has minor skin issues. His condition deteriorates, and he is sent to the LTACH on a ventilator with septicemia. In this example, the LTACH will assign a different DRG than the discharge DRG from the short-term acute hospital because generally the patient's condition has changed to warrant this extended stay. There are several examples in Figures 8.7–8.9 that show the short-term acute DRG and how the long-term care DRG (LTC-DRG) is associated with a different DRG, depending on the condition that extended the original stay in the hospital.

In the first example (Figure 8.7), the patient discharges from the short-term acute hospital with DRG 193, Simple Pneumonia and Pleurisy with MCC. Depending on the condition requiring an extended stay, the patient may have LTC-DRGs such as septicemia, renal failure, osteomyelitis or others. Similar examples are in Figures 8.8 and 8.9.

In Chapter 9, the issue of meaningful data is discussed. In today's world we have access to an exorbitant amount of data. The key is to ensure that the data are clear and concise and provide an accurate picture.

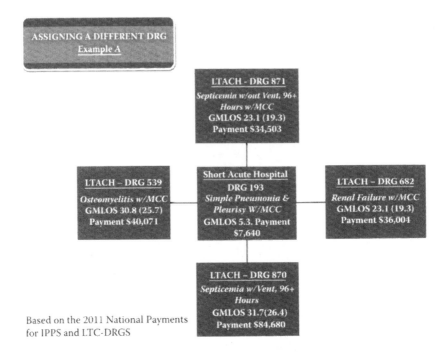

Based on the 2011 National Payments for IPPS and LTC-DRGS

FIGURE 8.7

Assigning a different DRG: Example A. (*Source:* Murer Consultants, Inc.)

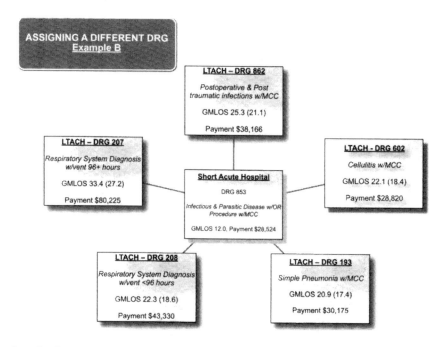

Source: Murer Consultants. Based on the 2011 National Payments for IPPS and LTC-DRGs.

FIGURE 8.8

Assigning a different DRG: Example B. (*Source:* Murer Consultants, Inc.)

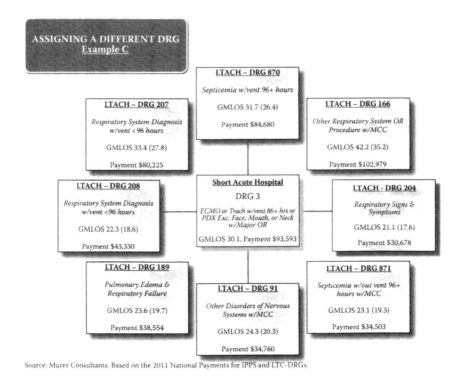

Source: Murer Consultants. Based on the 2011 National Payments for IPPS and LTC-DRGs.

FIGURE 8.9

Assigning a different DRG: Example C. (*Source:* Murer Consultants, Inc.)

CHAPTER 8 ACTION ITEMS

- Take a look at a typical diagnosis at your facility. Determine the DRG and the subcategories that could apply.
- Determine the comorbidities that qualify the patient to be assigned to a higher or lower DRG category based on CC/MCC or no CC/MCC

9

Meaningful Data

MEANINGFUL DATA

You are closely monitoring the average length of stay. You work with your physicians to ensure that the patient is moving through the continuum. You are using the working diagnosis-related group (DRG). You're confident your case management team is working together.

By all accounts it seems the patient is moving appropriately through the system, yet the numbers are not budging from last year's figures. The first place to look to determine why you're not seeing an impact might be your data.

EFFICACY OF DATA

With today's technology, health systems are suffering from information overload. One report may be generated by the finance department. A second report is based on the information obtained by patient services. The results don't match up, and in many instances these reports result in more questions than answers. Could it be possible these reports are based on flawed data? It is important for health systems to step back and assess how data are collected, disseminated, and interpreted. To be meaningful, data must provide a clear and concise picture.

For example, one facility determined that their inpatient days in the daily discharge report sometimes varied by more than 40 days per week, depending on the data that were included within the report. Prorated over one year, this discrepancy accounted for an additional 2,000 patient days.

A number of hospital departments—finance, patient services, and others—relied on these reports when compiling monthly statistical information including average length of stay, productivity reports, and others, which in some cases were based on inconsistent data.

ELECTRONIC MEDICAL RECORD

The patient medical record is a working document of patient care activity. The medical record is the primary means of communication about the patient's care among providers. In addition, the medical record is the key to proper reimbursement and serves as the legal document subject to access and review by patients, payers, regulatory bodies, insurers, and the court. For physicians, it is the best defense against a malpractice action.

The electronic health record should

- Improve patient care,
- Reduce errors,
- Reduce costs
- Streamline the healthcare delivery system.

Individuals will have state-to-state accessibility to their records. Electronic medical records will assist physicians with accurate and complete charting and help ensure all necessary entries are completed. The electronic medical record is a prime example of how clinical, regulatory, and financial issues intertwine.

In 2004, President George W. Bush stated all citizens would have access to the electronic medical record within 10 years. In February 2009, President Obama signed the American Recovery and Reinvestment Act (ARRA), which includes the HITECH Act (Health Information Technology for Economic and Clinical Health Act). HITECH's purpose is to promote the use of health information technology with a goal of utilization of an electronic health record for every person in the country by 2014.

The funding in this act is allocated to provide financial incentives to physicians, hospitals, and other healthcare providers to invest in information technology infrastructure, training, and the electronic health record.

On December 30, 2009, CMS released its notice of proposed rules implementing the ARRA of 2009 provisions providing incentive payments for the meaningful use of certified electronic health records technology. Providers and hospitals will be able to receive payments if they implement electronic health records and follow meaningful use criteria, which have been defined by this rule. The U.S. Department of Health and Human Services was charged through the ARRA to develop a program through which medical professionals would implement health information technology. Providers that participate in the Medicare and Medicaid programs stand to receive between $43,000 and $64,000 for individuals and up to $11 million for hospitals in case incentives over four to six years.

With these incentives, it is time for all health systems and physicians to transition to the electronic medical record. This change is needed to provide higher quality and more cost-effective healthcare. The electronic medical record allows for better tracking of injury and illness throughout the continuum of care. Hospitals and medical staff must collaborate together to create a workable unified electronic medical record system.

BENCHMARKS

Benchmarking in simplistic terms is the process by which you evaluate how your facility is doing in comparison with others. With benchmarking, the facility strives to improve quality of care. Benchmarks can incorporate a number of key areas including the following:

- Clinical
- Financial
- Regulatory

Each benchmark is intertwined with the others. Not a single positive result, but the combination of these results, leads to the success of the program. For example, if a hospital has a high case mix index, it would not be unusual for the hospital to have higher lab, radiology, and pharmacy charges. The higher case mix index should also reflect a higher reimbursement.

On the other hand, if the hospital has a lower case mix index yet has higher lab, radiology, and charges, there might be a problem. Benchmarks must be in sync with one another.

Benchmarks should be predetermined and closely monitored. They should be equally applied to the hospital and to the physician. Benchmarking including financial, clinical, and quality measures should help maintain accountability of operational and clinical performance. Table 9.1 is an example of benchmarks.

TABLE 9.1

Sample Benchmarks Working in Tandem

Acute Care Benchmark	Month 1	Month 2	Month 3	Average
Maintain a case mix index of 1.9 or greater of patient acuity				
Maintain an average length of stay of 5.5 days All Payer or 6.5 days Medicare				
Maintain a cost per patient day of $1250 or less				
Maintain medical supply ancillary services at $100 PPD or less				
Maintain pharmacy ancillary services at $135 PPD or less				
Maintain radiology ancillary services at $40 PPD or less				
Maintain average daily census as per budget				
Maintain direct nursing hours at target 7.25 DNH				
Minimize agency nursing to no more than 10% of total nursing staff				

Notes: Benchmarks should be in sync. For example, if there is a higher cost per day, you should see a higher case mix index.

PPD—Per Patient Day

DNH—Direct Nursing Hours

Source: Murer Consultants, Inc.

CHAPTER 9 ACTION ITEMS

- Where does your facility stand in the implementation of the electronic medical record?
- Assure benchmarks are in place for each venue of care within your continuum.

10

Conclusion

Case management is the necessary link in the chain that holds together an integrated healthcare delivery system. Effective use of the continuum of care ensures that each patient is treated at the right place for the right amount of time for the appropriate reimbursement and appropriate resource utilization.

Today's healthcare problems are complex and often cannot be solved from one single perspective. These problems don't come in tidy, separate packages; rather, they are intertwined. Thus, solutions must be comprehensive and address the whole puzzle, not just individual pieces.

Facilities need to implement aggressive campaigns to educate physicians, clinical staff, managed care payers, other referral sources, and even patients and their families as to what defines each post acute venue based on a product line model with clear definition of purpose and scope of services.

Admission criteria and protocols must be developed that are venue-specific to ensure the appropriate placement and movement of patients throughout the continuum of care. It is critical to educate clinical staff, physicians, and referral sources about admission criteria, protocols, and desired outcomes so that all involved are effectively utilizing available resources within the health system. Effective case management will play a vital role in the future success of a reformed healthcare delivery system.

Everyone involved in the case management team—nurses, physicians, case managers, and administrators—bears the responsibility to optimally utilize all resources for the primary purpose of ensuring strength and availability of the health system in perpetuity. If not, we won't have a system to protect.

An integrated healthcare system must come together to ensure that each patient is treated at the right place for the right amount of time for the appropriate reimbursement.

In today's tempestuous times, healthcare providers must navigate the waters with neither pessimism nor fear, but rather with a strong dose of practicability and pragmatism.

11

Examination Questions

1. Are all patients assigned a case manager?
2. How do you identify patients who may potentially need post acute services?
3. What criteria do you use in deciding which post acute venue is most appropriate?
4. At what point in a patient's hospital stay are you able to work with discharge planning and begin the post acute placement process?
5. Identify the primary obstacles in performing your duties.
6. List the primary roadblocks that jeopardize a timely discharge to the next venue.
7. Define *your role* in the case management process from your own perspective and share how it might differ from the expectations of the organization.
8. How do you deal with individuals who are noncompliant?
9. What is the interaction between the case management team at your facility?
   - Case manager to nurse
   - Case manager to physician
   - Nurse to physician
   - Nurse to administration
10. To whom do you owe your highest duty and responsibility as a case manager?

12

Class Exercises

EXERCISE 1: DEVELOP A VENUE INVENTORY WORKSHEET

A venue inventory worksheet should list all the venues within your hospital or health system, as well as available venues within the community.

Once venues have been identified, the class should work to develop a detailed sheet highlighting key areas of each venue, including the following:

- Venue purpose
- Number of beds (if applicable)
- Anticipated length of stay
- Reimbursement structure
- Regulatory requirements

EXERCISE 2: IDENTIFY THE PARAMETERS OF CASE MANAGEMENT IN YOUR ORGANIZATION

- What are the roles and responsibilities of your case management team?
- What type of case management system is your organization currently utilizing?
- Do all case managers share a common language, regulatory knowledge, and so forth to assist with informed decision making regarding full utilization of the health system's continuum of care?

EXERCISE 3: KEY OBSTACLES

Identify all key obstacles at your facility to moving patients appropriately in a timely manner to the most appropriate level of care based on each patient's medical necessity. Once these obstacles are identified, develop strategies to reduce or eliminate issues causing the untimely movement of patients.

EXERCISE 4: OPPORTUNITIES FOR EFFECTIVE USE OF POST ACUTE VENUES OF CARE

Discuss your options in moving the patient from the most expensive level of care to the most appropriate post acute venue. Discuss the importance of choosing the most appropriate venue based on the patient's medical necessity.

EXERCISE 5: CASE MANAGEMENT IN A MULTIVENUE SETTING

Understand the appropriate use of each post acute venue. Develop discharge triggers to establish seamless protocols from one venue to the next.

Appendix A: Glossary

arithmetic mean length of stay (AMLOS): The average number of days patients within a given DRG stay in the hospital; also referred to as the average length of stay. The AMLOS is used to determine payment for outlier cases.

average length of stay (ALOS): This is the statistic used by hospitals to determine the average number of days between admission and discharge.

base rate: The hospital's base rate is a number assigned to calculate DRG reimbursement. The rate varies by hospital based on a number of issues including each facility's location, rural/urban designation, and labor costs. This base rate is used in determining individual DRG payments.

bundling payment or bundled payment: The use of a single payment for a group of related services.

CMS: Centers for Medicare and Medicaid Services.

case mix group (CMG): The patient classification system for inpatient rehabilitation patients who are expected to have similar resource utilization needs and outcomes. The data entered on the patient assessment instrument (PAI) is used to classify a patient into a specific CMG.

case mix index (CMI): The total of all the DRG relative weights, divided by the number of Medicare discharges.

complication/comorbidity (CC): A condition that, when present, leads to substantially increased hospital resource utilization. May require additional caregivers.

comprehensive inpatient rehabilitation (CIR): A Medicare-recognized venue providing comprehensive inpatient rehabilitation services. Under federal regulations, patients admitted to these facilities must be medically stable, able to tolerate a minimum of three hours of therapy per day, and a percentage must fall within specific rehabilitation diagnosis.

continuum of care: The various levels of care that provide the most appropriate care based on the patient's medical necessity and resource allocation.

diagnosis-related group (DRG): One of the 746 categories that classifies a patient into clinical groups that demonstrate similar consumption of hospital resources and length of stay patterns.

discharge: The release of a patient from an inpatient facility after receiving treatment.

excluded hospital: Hospitals excluded from the federal inpatient prospective payment system (IPPS) include psychiatric hospitals and units, rehabilitation hospitals and units, children's hospitals, long-term acute care hospitals, and cancer hospitals.

geometric mean length of stay (GMLOS): Used to compute reimbursement, the GMLOS is a statistically adjusted value for all cases for a given DRG, allowing for the outliers, transfer cases, and negative outlier cases that would normally skew the data. The GMLOS is used to determine transfer case per diem rates.

high cost outlier (HCO): A case in which the cost of care is much higher than similar cases. A high cost outlier payment is applied to cover these higher-than-anticipated costs based on a specific formula.

home health: Skilled nursing and therapeutic services generally provided in the home.

hospice: A venue offering palliative care and support services that address the physical, spiritual, social, and economic needs of a terminally ill patient and the patient's family. Hospice can be provided at home or at hospice facilities.

ICD-9-CM: International Classification of Diseases, 9th Revision, Clinical Modification; the code that characterizes the underlying impairment conditions for which the patient is being treated

inpatient prospective payment system (IPPS): Medicare's payment system using DRGs to determine hospital reimbursement. Each DRG has a payment assigned to it, based on the average resources used to treat the Medicare patient under that DRG.

long-term acute care hospital (LTACH): An acute care hospital recognized by 42 CFR§412.23 (e) whose Medicare patients have an average length of stay greater than 25 days. LTACHs generally provide diagnostic and medical treatment to patients with chronic and complex medical conditions.

major complication/comorbidity (MCC): Diagnosis codes that reflect the highest level of severity (see also Complication/Comborbiditity).

major diagnostic category (MDC): Broad classification of diagnoses typically grouped by body system.

Medicare: A federal program that reimburses providers for healthcare services for individuals 65 and older, people with disabilities, and those with end-stage renal disease. Part A reimburses hospital programs, and Part B reimburses physicians and other services.

Medicaid: A program that reimburses providers for expenses incurred in the treatment of individuals with low incomes and limited resources. Benefits can vary from state to state.

MedPAC: Medicare Payment Advisory Commission; an independent federal body established to advise the U.S. Congress on issues affecting the Medicare program.

Methicillin-resistant *Staphylococcus aureus* (MRSA): A bacterial infection that is highly resistant to a number of antibiotics.

relative weight: An assigned weight that is intended to reflect the relative resource consumption associated with each DRG. The higher the relative weight, the greater the payment to the hospital.

resource utilization group (RUG): Classification system used by skilled nursing facilities to determine payment.

skilled nursing unit (SNU): Facility or unit that provides skilled nursing care to patients who require medical or nursing care or rehabilitation to patients who are injured, disabled, or ill. Can also be referred to as a skilled nursing facility (SNF).

short stay outlier (SSO): A case in which the patient stays less than the anticipated length of stay, causing a reduction in the full payment.

transfer: The move of a patient to another acute care hospital for related care.

Appendix B: Acronyms and Abbreviations

AAPM&R	American Academy of Physical Medicine and Rehabilitation
ACE	Acute Care Episode
AHA	American Hospital Association
AMLOS	Arithmetic Mean Length of Stay
ARRA	American Recovery and Reinvestment Act
BBA	Balanced Budget Act
CARF	Commission on Accreditation of Rehabilitation Facilities
CBO	Congressional Budget Office
CC	Complication/Comorbidity
CIR	Comprehensive Inpatient Rehabilitation
CMG	Case Mix Group
CMI	Case Mix Index
CMS	Centers for Medicare and Medicaid Services
CORF	Comprehensive Outpatient Rehabilitation Facility
CPT	Current Procedural Technology
DNH	Direct Nursing Hours
DRG	Diagnosis-Related Group
EHR	Electronic Health Record
FY	Fiscal Year
GDP	Gross Domestic Product
GMLOS	Geometric Mean Length of Stay
HCO	High Cost Outlier
HFMA	Healthcare Financial Management Association
HHA	Home Health Agency
HITECH	Health Information Technology for Economic and Clinical Health Act
ICD-9-CM	International Classification of Disease, 9th Revision for Clinical Management
ICU	Intensive Care Unit
IPPS	Inpatient Prospective Payment System
IRF	Inpatient Rehabilitation Facility

LPN	Licensed Practical Nurse
LTACH	Long-Term Acute Care Hospital
LTC-DRG	Long-Term Care Diagnosis-Related Group
MCC	Major Complication/Comorbidity
MDC	Major Diagnostic Category
MDS	Minimum Data Set
MRSA	Methicillin Resistant *Staphylococcus Aureus*
PAC	Post Acute Care
PAI	Patient Assessment Instrument
PPD	Per Patient Day
PPS	Prospective Payment System
RAC	Recover Audit Contractors
RUG	Resource Utilization Group
SNF	Skilled Nursing Facility
SNU	Skilled Nursing Unit
SSO	Short Stay Outlier

Index

Printed and bound by CPI Group (UK) Ltd, Croydon, CR0 4YY

25/10/2024

01779633-0002